High

GATEWAY TO
ITALIAN ART SONGS

*An Anthology of Italian Song
and Interpretation*

John Glenn Paton

Cover photo: A gate to the Borghese Gardens, Rome.
Photo by John Glenn Paton.

Now a public park, the gardens are on land acquired during
the 1600s by Cardinal Scipione Borghese. Near this gate
is the Villa Borghese, a palatial structure that was not a
residence, but an art gallery and a center for festivities.
The Villa now houses an important collection of paintings, as
well as sculptures by Gian Lorenzo Bernini.

Copyright © MMIV by Alfred Music Publishing Co., Inc.
All Rights Reserved.   Printed In USA.
ISBN-10: 0-7390-3547-9 (Book)
ISBN-13: 978-0-7390-3547-4 (Book)
ISBN-10: 0-7390-3548-7 (Book & 2CDs)
ISBN-13: 978-0-7390-3548-1 (Book & 2CDs)

D0524646

Table of Contents

About This Edition

The title, *Gateway to Italian Art Songs*, embraces what Italians call *musica vocale da camera*, that is, songs written for the home or concert hall, not for the church (*musica da chiesa*) or opera (*musica da teatro*).

The story of *musica vocale da camera* begins in the same time and place as the history of opera, with the often told story of the Camerata of Florence. This volume begins with the next generation, the cantata composers who flourished in Rome in the mid-1600s. The story continues with selections from the Baroque to the early 1900s. This is the first anthology that offers a "gateway" for singers to explore beyond the early music with which their study customarily begins into the Romantic songs of the *bel canto* composers and beyond.

Our constant goal— artistic communication with an audience— can only be accomplished when a singer clearly understands the message and meaning of the song. The commentary pages before each song help with the preparatory steps that should come before actual singing: translating and analyzing the text and researching the historical background of both text and music.

Because these songs come from manuscripts and from publishers in several countries it is necessary to impose uniformity on them without altering them significantly. Modern clefs are used, small note values are beamed together, and obvious misprints are corrected without any special notice.

Throughout the book, slurs are used in the modern way to indicate that a sung syllable extends over more than one note. In works composed after 1800 dotted slurs are used to show where composers placed slurs for other reasons, e.g., to show expressive legato, to mark breath phrasing, or to indicate a *portamento* between two notes.

If the original sources contain ornaments, they are reproduced exactly here. If they are ambiguous, the correct performance is suggested in a footnote. In the 1600s, singers may have improvised vocal ornaments more or less constantly and intuitively. However, historical sources state that *musica da camera* should be ornamented much less than operatic music. Certainly, composers after 1800 wrote out the ornaments they wanted, and one should seldom add more.

Tempos in Italian music are seldom metronomic, but metronome markings are suggested as starting points. Italian tempo and style markings are translated in an appendix at the back of the book.

Song texts have been edited for uniformity; spelling is modernized. In older sources words and syllables were often written carelessly or spaced incorrectly under the notes, resulting in inappropriate accentuation. Italian singers would simply correct such errors at sight, as they have been corrected here.

The first word of a line of verse is capitalized when it is printed in verse form, but not when the text is printed with music.

Old manuscripts typically had no more punctuation than a period at the end of the aria. Even in printed music, punctuation was not standardized before the 1900s. I have punctuated the texts in a modern style to clarify the meanings of the texts.

Some written punctuation signs stand for breaths but others do not. The difference is found only by reading the poem aloud. I have inserted two kinds of phrase markings above the vocal line:

1) $\lor$, where the musical line must be interrupted in order to articulate the text correctly;

2) ᾽ where a breath may be taken if it is needed for convenience.

Practicing with the CDs

Coordinated with this book are two CDs containing all of the piano accompaniments, artistically recorded by Joan Thompson, pianist, under my close supervision. The performances are intended to be expressive and faithful to the composers' wishes, while avoiding extreme interpretations that could be misleading to students. The recordings are a learning tool that is meant to be used until you have the opportunity to enjoy the collaboration of a live pianist. They cannot substitute for the excitement of interactive music making, and you should not feel that you must adhere to their exact tempos and nuances in your own real performances.

In songs without an introduction, you will hear your opening pitch played on the piano several times in the tempo of the first measure. Also, if there is a difficult entrance after a pause in the music, the piano may play the next notes of the voice part and then continue with the accompaniment.

Sources

The commentary before each song states where it was found (except for published songs that are in my personal collection).   Thanks are due to the foundations and governments that maintain these treasures and to the staff members who helped me access them.   In the commentaries, libraries are identified by their cities, as follows:

Berlin: Staatsbibliothek preussischer Kulturbesitz,
    Musikabteilung;

Brussels: Bibliothèque Royale Albert Ier;

Budapest: Research Library for Music History,
    Franz Liszt Academy of Music;

London: British Library;

Los Angeles: University of California,
    Walter H. Rubsamen Music Library;

Milan: Biblioteca del Conservatorio di Musica
    'Giuseppe Verdi,' Dr. Agostina Laterza, librarian;

Naples: Biblioteca del Conservatorio di
    San Pietro a Majella;

New York: Mary Flagler Cary Music Collection of
    The Pierpont Morgan Library;

Paris: Bibliothèque Nationale;

Regensburg: Bischöfliche Zentralbibliothek;

Rochester: Eastman School of Music Library;

Rome: Biblioteca Musicale Governativa del
    Conservatorio di Musica di S. Cecilia;

Vatican: Biblioteca Apostolica Vaticana;

Vienna: Oesterreichische Nationalbibliothek.

Appreciation is also due to the Music Library of the University of Southern California, Rodney Rolfs, Librarian, where much basic reading was done.

Every writer about music must acknowledge the rich resources of *The New Grove Dictionary of Music and Musicians*. Another important reference work is known by the acronym of its publisher, UTET; its full name is *Dizionario enciclopedico universale della musica e dei musicisti* (Turin, 1985).

Acknowledgments

Joan Thompson, my wife, often passed up the usual pleasures of vacations in Paris and Rome.   Instead, she shared in the excitement of discovering songs and spent hours copying scores by hand when we were not allowed to photocopy them. I am grateful for her unending enthusiasm and support, her musical insights, and her careful proofreading and editorial suggestions.

Prof. Luigi Marzola of the Conservatorio di Musica 'G. Verdi,' Milan, worked closely with me to resolve questions about the phonetics and translations. His musical and linguistic insights were invaluable (but any errors that may remain are mine, not his).

Valuable musical insights came from harpsichordist Roswitha Klotz and cellist Udo Klotz, who performed the Rossi and Scarlatti cantatas with me in Regensburg, Germany.

Among the talented professionals at Alfred Publishing Co., I would particularly like to acknowledge the guidance of Karen Surmani and the masterful layout design by Bruce Goldes.

If this *Gateway* is successful, it will awaken young singers' curiosity and provide some of the necessary tools to explore more Italian art songs, especially reaching into the rich repertoire of the 1900s, the songs of Ottorino Respighi, Francesco Cilea, Barbara Giuranna, Luigi Dallapiccola and many others.

John Glenn Paton
Los Angeles

The Composers and Their Times

The Baroque Era

In Florence, in the years leading up to 1600, there was a revolutionary innovation, a new style of singing in the rhythms and inflections of speech, accompanied by simple chords. This "new music," directly appealing to the emotions, made opera possible and opened the way to a new style, which we call Baroque.

Parallel to the development of opera was a more intimate art, that of the solo cantata, which became the dominant form of chamber music in Baroque Italy. The first masters of the solo cantata were in Rome, where they wrote for professional singers. Thousands of their unpublished solo cantatas survive in handsomely bound manuscripts in European libraries, attesting that singers and their employers were eager to have new works in this favored medium.

The solo cantata was an elegant art form, intended for a classically educated audience. The aristocracy of Rome included cardinals of the Church, descendants and relatives of popes, and Queen Christina of Sweden, who left her Lutheran country in 1654 to become a Catholic. Rivalry among such patrons meant employment for many musicians and composers. Private performances were desirable because public theaters were seasonal at best and were often closed by papal order for years at a time.

Women seldom sang in public in Rome. Most solo vocal works were written for male soprano voices, with a typical range from middle C to A above the staff. Others were written for male altos, but almost none for changed male voices.

The musical techniques used in cantatas developed in a way parallel to those of opera. From short movements loosely linked together, as in the works of Rossi and Savioni, there was a change toward a strict separation between the functions of recitative and aria.

In both operas and cantatas the favorite aria form came to be the *da capo aria*. It consisted of a *prima parte* (first part), a contrasting *seconda parte* (second part), and a *da capo* (from the top) repetition of the *prima parte*. Baroque theorists justified the validity of the formula: They said that a human being can hold onto a strong feeling (*prima parte*) for only a limited time before it changes in some way (*seconda parte*), after which the first emotion can return (*da capo*) with renewed vigor.

Just as aria forms became more standardized, so did the sequence of movements in cantatas. If R stands for recitative and A for aria, a typical form might be ARA, RARA, or a similar variant of these.

Performance: The Singer

Italian Baroque music always presupposes a beautiful voice, excellent technique, dramatic intention, and an expressive delivery of a poetic text. Even the most intense emotions are expressed within a framework of dignity and courtly restraint, but in that context the singer is allowed many liberties. Tempos may be flexible in a piece which has slow chord changes and long bass tones, or strict in a livelier piece. Composers did not indicate dynamics, but performers must have used dynamic variety as an essential element of dramatic impact.

Even before 1600, books of vocal ornaments showed how to vary music, especially at a final cadence. If a song ended with the pitches *re* and *do* on long notes, a competent singer would always replace the *re* with one of many melodic formulas or with a trill, at least. Such variations called to the important cadence points. Smaller ornaments, such as grace notes and passing tones, could occur spontaneously in nearly every phrase, especially in slow tempos.

A popular vocal ornament in the early 1600s was the *trillo*, a rapid repetition of notes on a single pitch. What we now call a trill, the rapid alternation of two pitches a step apart, was then known as a *gruppetto* (little group). Later in the 1600s the repetitive *trillo* became less fashionable and the alternating trill became common. (Ornaments suggested by the editor of this book are shown by notes with small heads; they are not obligatory.)

The late Baroque required some minor changes of technique. The repetitive *trillo* went out of style, but other ornaments remained in common use. Singers maintained interest through the many *da capo* arias by taking each part of the aria to a different expressive level. They were criticized if they did not ornament the repetition of the *prima parte* imaginatively. (However, ornamentation in *musica da camera* was probably less elaborate than in operatic arias.)

Recitatives challenge the singer to sing accurate pitches and rhythms and yet convey the impression of natural speech inflections. The singer must be both a fine musician and a fine actor.

In recitatives, the singer must know when to use an *appoggiatura* (leaning note): If the first of two identical notes is stressed, the singer usually should change it to the scale tone above (sometimes even higher, or sometimes the tone below). Being dissonant with the bass, an *appoggiatura* adds expressive emphasis to the stressed syllable. In other words, the composer expected to hear the stressed dissonant tones but wrote the notes that would show the continuo player what chords to play. In this book, the letter name of the appoggiatural note is printed above the note to which it resolves.

Performance: The Keyboard Player

The first eight composers in this book, including Pergolesi, used a shorthand-like method of composition: They wrote only the voice and bass parts, and they relied on the instrumentalist to know what chords to play. The usual chord instruments were harpsichord, guitar or lute, and the bass part was also played on a cello, bass viol or other instrument.

The bass part, called a *basso continuo*, could be marked with a sharp sign for a major chord, a flat for a minor chord, or numbers to indicate inverted chords, but many scores contain no such signs. Modern editions provide a "realization" that notates the keyboard part in detail.

If the bass part of a Baroque song has a melodic character, it should be brought out as a counterpoint to the voice. The chords added by the editor can be tailored to the requirements of the singer, the instrument and the acoustics of the room. The player may decide: 1) to double the bass notes an octave lower or higher, 2) to add or omit chord tones or change their octave location, 3) to support the singer with repeated chords, or 4) to double the singer's notes if necessary.

A peculiarity of later Baroque recitatives is that the end of a vocal phrase may clash with the playing of a full cadence. In that case, the cadence is usually played after the singer finishes, causing an extra beat or two in the measure. Such cadences are shown with broken lines in this book.

Luigi Rossi
(Torremaggiore, c1597-Rome,1653)

Rossi grew up at the royal court of Naples and learned music there until he entered the service of the Borghese family in Rome. Rossi married a famous harpist, and at age 36 he became the organist of the church of San Luigi dei Francesi. He later served Cardinal Barberini, who commissioned his first opera, *Il palazzo incantato*. He was respected above all for his more than 300 solo cantatas, which are richly varied melodically and formally.

Mario Savioni
(Rome, 1608-Rome, 1685)

As a boy soprano Savioni sang in the choir of St. Peter's Basilica in the Vatican. Little is known about his adult life, but he sang as a male alto at Rossi's church and sang a secondary role in Rossi's opera.

Alessandro Scarlatti
(Palermo, 1660–Naples, 1725)

Born into a family of singers and composers, Scarlatti and two of his sisters were taken to Rome for their musical education. Before his 18th birthday, he had married and composed his first opera. After finding success in Rome, he entered the service of the viceroy of Naples and wrote at least 32 operas during his first years there. As Scarlatti matured and wrote in a more learned style, audiences turned toward composers whose music was simpler and more tuneful.

A basic research tool was compiled by Edwin Hanley in *Alessandro Scarlatti's Cantate da camera: A Bibliographical Study* (dissertation, Yale University, 1963).

When pianists speak of Scarlatti, they usually mean Alessandro's oldest son Domenico, whose works appear often on piano recitals.

Francesco Bartolomeo Conti
(Florence, 1681-Vienna, 1732)

The mandolin and theorbo, a long-necked lute, were the instruments that Conti played in his international career and featured in the operas that he composed. Employed as a theorbist at the imperial court in Vienna, Conti rose to the position of court composer. His second and third wives were *prime donne* of the court opera. His musical experimentation helped music to evolve toward the Classical style.

Francesco Durante
(Frattamaggiore, 1684-Naples, 1755)

Taught music by an uncle who was an experienced composer, Durante spent most of his life in Naples, working in various churches and teaching positions. His students loved him and revered him as a learned arbiter in all questions of musical theory.

Giovanni Battista Pergolesi
(Iesi, 1710-Pozzuoli/Naples 1736)

First as a choirboy and then as a violinist, Pergolesi earned his tuition at a conservatory in Naples and studied with Francesco Durante. His comic intermezzo *La serva padrona* was performed all over Europe and became a model for comic operas, and he created a handful of other superb works, including a *Stabat Mater* for women's voices. After his early death, many works were falsely attributed to him.

Classical Era

The transition from Baroque to Classical was gradual and evolutionary, but nonetheless clear to those who lived through it. Around 1750 the word "baroque" was first used as an insult: it came from the word for a bulbous, irregularly formed pearl, and it was used to imply that the art of the preceding generations was unnatural, complicated, ostentatious and unbalanced. The new music of the time aimed to imitate the "classical" art of ancient Greece, in being natural, simple, modest and symmetrical.

A major change in musical style was that vocal music was composed with fully written out keyboard parts. Bass parts seldom had melodic interest, and they were often reduced to repetitiously playing the roots of the harmonies.

Solo cantatas went out of style, replaced by concert arias with orchestral accompaniment. Solo songs returned to popularity in Italy after 1800 in the form of the *romanza*, borrowing the name of a French song type called *romance*. Rather than an elite art performed by professionals for the delight of aristocrats, the *romanza* was intended for amateurs who could afford pianos in their homes.

Vincenzo Righini
(Bologna, 1756-Bologna, 1812)

At age 20 Righini already belonged to an opera company in Prague, but he had little success as a tenor and perhaps had a damaged voice. He turned to operatic composition and wrote an opera, *Il convitato di pietra* (1776), based on the story that Mozart later used in Don Giovanni. Most of his career as a composer and singing teacher was spent in German-speaking cities. In his last illness he returned to Italy and died after surgery in Bologna.

Isabella Colbran-Rossini, born Isabel Ángeles Colbrán
(Madrid, Spain, 1785-Castenaso/Bologna,1845)

The daughter of a violinist in the Royal Orchestra in Madrid, Colbran composed and published a book of Italian songs when she was 14. She is said to have sung at the crowning of Napoleon as Emperor in 1804. She sang at La Scala in Milan in 1808 and dominated the opera at Naples for more than a decade. Rossini composed leading roles for her, lived with her, and married her in 1822, but they later separated. She published four books of songs.

Nicola Vaccai
(Tolentino, 1790-Pesaro, 1848)

As a teenager, Vaccai was an accomplished poet. While studying law in Rome, he discovered a talent for musical composition. After studying with Paisiello in Naples, he composed for major opera houses, but his real gift was for graceful melody rather than dramatic impact. Vaccai was always in demand as a singing teacher, especially in high society. His *Metodo pratico* (Practical Method), written in London in 1833, is still used by voice students. He later headed the Milan conservatory. His son Giulio wrote his biography.

Gioachino Rossini
(Pesaro, 1792-Passy, France, 1868)

After Rossini's parents settled in Bologna, he had opportunities as a boy singer on stage, as a composer, and as a keyboard player in theaters. Ambitious and industrious, he produced his eighteenth opera just before his 24th birthday; it was *Il barbiere di Siviglia*, one of the greatest of all comic operas. *Guillaume Tell* (1829), still famous for its overture, was his last opera. He had earned his financial security, and he lived in Paris, admired for his witty conversation, but was often in poor health.

Romantic Era

Romanticism as an artistic movement originated in the northern countries, Britain, France and Germany. It came to Italy later than to other countries, perhaps because Italian operas had always portrayed extreme emotions, improbable coincidences, and exotic scenes in the remote past. A quintessential Romantic opera was Donizetti's *Lucia di Lammermoor*, which has all of those features.

In the field of song, the Romantic era meant a steady production of *romanze*, including such types as the *barcarola*, resembling a Venetian boat-song, and the *canzonetta*, resembling a folksong. Donizetti and Bellini published *ariette*, an old term which retained its elegance. Beginning in the 1840s, Italian composers borrowed a French word, *mélodie*, or in Italian, *melodia*, to describe songs of greater seriousness and complexity.

Gaetano Donizetti
(Bergamo, 1797-Bergamo, 1848)

Born into the deepest poverty, the young Donizetti received the charitable care of a highly respected German born composer, Simon Mayr. Talent and hard work brought him an international career, but his personal life was blighted by the deaths of his young wife and their three children. He had unusual success with both comic and tragic subjects; *L'elisir d'amore*, *Lucia di Lammermoor*, *La fille du régiment* and *Don Pasquale* are all part of today's operatic repertoire.

Vincenzo Bellini
(Catania, 1801-Puteaux/Paris,1835)

Bellini learned piano from his father and composition from his grandfather. He studied further in Naples and achieved his first great success with *Il Pirata* (1827). *I Capuleti e i Montecchi* was also sung internationally, but often with Vaccai's version of the final scene. *Norma* (1831) is now admired above any of his other operas. He died of an intestinal ailment, complicated by medical malpractice.

Marietta Brambilla
(Cassano d'Adda, 1807-Milan, 1875)

Marietta was the oldest of five Brambilla sisters, all of whom had operatic careers. A true contralto, she made her debut in London in 1827 and specialized in trouser roles, some of which were written for her by Donizetti. She married a nobleman in 1856. After his death four years later, she devoted herself to teaching and composition.

Giuseppe Verdi
(Le Róncole, near Busseto, 1813-Milan, 1901)

Born into a poor peasant family, Verdi studied privately, not at the Milan conservatory that later honored him by taking his name. He rose by his own labors to become the greatest Italian composer of his century. He was also a public spokesman for Italian independence and a senator in the first Italian parliament. The income from his estate built and still supports a home for retired musicians in Milan.

Luigi Arditi
(Crescentino, 1822-Hove, England, 1903)

Having already shown talent and leadership in his hometown, Arditi entered the Milan conservatory at age 14 and studied composition with Vaccai. A talented conductor who led an orchestra by playing the violin, he toured in Cuba and the United States and married an American woman, Virginia Warwick. He conducted in many cities, and in London he led the British premieres of many important operas. A great storyteller, he published *My Reminiscences* in 1896.

Amilcare Ponchielli
(Paderno Fasolaro/Cremona, 1834-Milan, 1886)

Ponchielli left Cremona to study at the Milan conservatory, but he had to return home to find work. His ambitions for a larger career suffered many false starts and disappointments. His first great success was *I promessi sposi* when he was 38. It was followed by *La Gioconda*, the only one of his operas that had success outside Italy. He married Teresina Brambilla, a niece and student of Marietta Brambilla.

Francesco Paolo Tosti
(Ortano sul Mare, 1846-Rome, 1916)

After studying music in Naples, Tosti moved to Rome in 1870 to introduce himself as a singer and composer. Success came when Princess Margherita of Savoia (later Queen of Italy) engaged him as her singing teacher. In 1880 he settled in England and became the singing teacher to the royal family. Tosti and his wife Berthe were close friends of Puccini, especially when all three lived for a time in the same hotel in Rome. Tosti composed more than 350 songs to texts in Italian, English and French.

Ruggero Leoncavallo
(Naples, 1857-Montecatini, 1919)

Until age 18 Leoncavallo studied music in Naples and literature in Bologna. From this background he wrote his own texts for most of his operas and songs. He had only one lasting success, *Pagliacci* (1892). His setting of *La Bohème* was initially successful but did not survive in competition with Puccini's. He was working on projects for the Chicago Lyric Opera when he died.

Giacomo Puccini
(Lucca, 1858-Brussels, 1924)

Four generations of Puccinis were leading musicians in Lucca. Giacomo studied with Ponchielli at the Milan conservatory. In his 20s he won the support of the powerful publisher Giulio Ricordi, who groomed him for a long series of successes from *Manon Lescaut* (1891) to the posthumous *Turandot* (completed by Alfano, 1926).

Gabriele Sibella

Ironically, the last composer in our collection is the one about whom we know the least. A publisher in St. Petersburg, Russia, brought out three of his French songs in 1909. G. Schirmer, New York, published 18 of his songs in Italian, seven in French and one in English.

Anime voi
/aːnime voi/
You Souls Who Are

Luigi Rossi (c1597–1653)
/luiːdʒi rosːsi/

aːnime voi ke seːte
1. **Anime voi, che sete**
Souls   you, who are

dalːle fuːrje dabisːso oppresːseoɲːɲoːra
2. **Dalle furie d'abisso oppresse ̑ogn'ora,**
by-the Furies of-Abyss oppressed every-hour,

kredeːte‿a me kredeːte
3. **Credete ̑a me, credete**
believe – me, believe

ke kwel mal ke   vakːkoːra
4. **Che quel mal che   v'accora**
that that evil which you-afflicts

ɛun ombra delːle peːne e del doloːre
5. **È un ombra delle pene e del dolore**
is a shadow of-the pains and of-the sorrow

ke dʒeloːzo aːmator sofːfre in amoːre
6. **Che geloso ̑amator soffre in amore.**
which jealous lover   suffers in love.

ki   non sa ke koːza siːa
7. **Chi non sa che cosa sia**
Whoever does-not know what thing is

dʒeloziːa lo kjɛːda   me
8. **Gelosia, lo chied'a   me;**
jealousy, it may-he-ask-of me;

lo dimandi alːlalma   miːa
9. **Lo dimandi   all'alma   mia,**
it he-may-ask of-the-soul mine,

lo sapraː   dalːla miːa fe
10. **Lo saprà   dalla mia fé,**
it he-will-know from my faith,

ke diranːno kuːn afːfanːno
11. **Che diranno ch'un affanno,**
which will-say that-an anxiety,

un tormento‿un krutːtʃo‿etɛrno
12. **Un tormento, ̑un cruccio ̑eterno,**
a torment, a worry eternal,

un purgatoːrjo‿alfin pɛdːdʒo ɛ dinfɛrno
13. **Un purgatorio ̑alfin peggio è d'inferno.**
a purgatory finally worse is than-hell.

taːle‿apːpunto lo prɔːvo
14. **Tale ̑appunto lo provo**
Such, exactly, it I-experience

kidolatrando   uːna beltà diviːna
15. **Ch'idolatrando una beltà divina,**
because,-idolizing a   beauty divine,

io tɛːmo koɲːɲi zgwardo
16. **Io temo ch'ogni sguardo**
I fear that-every gaze

damantɛ insidjator non siːa   rapaːtʃe
17. **D'amante insidiator non sia   rapace**
of-love treacherous not might-be predatory

per involar kwel bɛl ke si mi pjatʃe
18. **Per involar quel bel   che sì mi piace.**
to abduct that beauty who so me pleases.

mindʃeloziʃːʃe‿unastro
19. **M'ingelosisce   un'astro,**
me-makes-jealous a-star,

mi turba oɲːɲi pjaneːta
20. **Mi turba ̑ogni pianeta.**
me upsets every planet.

tɛːmo kil tʃɛːlo istesːso
21. **Temo ch'il cielo ̑istesso**
I-fear that-the Heaven itself

non me   lo tɔlga un di
22. **Non me   lo tolga ̑un dí,**
not from-me takes-away one day,

inːnamoraːto‿aŋkesːso
23. **Innamorato ̑anch'esso**
in-love,   also-it,

del bɛl ke mi feːri
24. **Del bel che mi ferí.**
of-the beauty that me wounded.

di kimɛːre di fantaːzme
25. **Di chimere e di fantasme**
By chimeras and by fantasms

ɔ la mentɛ instupidiːta
26. **Ho la mente ̑instupidita;**
I-have a mind stunned;

pjɛːnɔ il   kor di dɔʎːʎe spazmi
27. **Pieno ho il cor di doglie e spasmi;**
full I-have a heart with pains and spasms;

sta fra krutːtʃi la miːa viːta
28. **Sta fra crucci la mia vita.**
is between worries — my life.

oɲːɲombra madombra
29. **Ogn'ombra m'adombra,**
Every-shadow me-makes-suspicious,

il kɔːre mabːbaʎːʎa
30. **Il core m'abbaglia,**
the heart me-deludes,

ne maj da me zgombra
31. **Ne mai da me sgombra**
nor ever from me clears

si fjɛːra batːtaʎːʎa
32. **Sí fiera battaglia.**
such fierce battle.

onde kintormentarmi
33. **Onde   ch'intormentarmi**
Therefore, that to-torment-myself

forsɛːkio diːkalfin in fjɔːke karmi
34. **Fors'è ch'io dica alfin' in fiochi carmi:**
perhaps-it-is I-say finally in feeble songs:
Chi non sa, etc.

Poetic Background

"You who know nothing about jealousy can learn from me. It is on my mind night and day." Jealousy is one of the favorite topics of cantata texts, and this poem explores varying moods of jealousy in some detail.

Line 1: *sete*, an obsolete form of *siete*, has a closed vowel [e].

Line 2: *furie*, in Greek mythology, are three fearful winged females with snakes in their hair, who punish wrongdoers; *d'abisso* refers to Tartarus, where the Furies live, a place of punishment located below Hades.

Line 13: *peggio è d'inferno* is repeated, omitting the verb *è* once it has been expressed.

Line 18: *quel bel* is masculine, meaning "that which attracts by its beauty." Although grammatically masculine, it refers to the beloved woman.

Lines 19-20: *astro...pianeta* refers to the beliefs of astrology, which was very popular in Rossi's time, that stars and planets are forces that can affect us.

Line 22: *lo* refers to *bel* in line 18, i.e., the woman.

Line 23: *anch'esso*, even Heaven.

Line 34: *carmi* (singular, *il carme*, from Latin *carmen*, song) are lyric poems.

Musical Background

The music of this splendid cantata mirrors a jealous person's constantly changing states of mind. The singer begins by calling the damned souls in Hell to witness that their pains are not as bad as the pains of a jealous lover. *"Soffre"* releases a torrent of scales (m11–13), before the principal aria, *"Chi non sa..."* makes a calmer statement (m16). Another recitative (m39) begins quietly, quickly increases in intensity, and leads to a pair of movements (beginning in m54 and m63) that give vent to the lover's anger and resentment. In a brief recitative the singer says that he finds relief in singing, *"Chi non sa..."*

In 1646 Rossi visited visited Paris to write an opera for the royal court. At that time a gentleman in Paris sent a copy of *"Anime voi..."* to a friend in Holland. We do not know whether Rossi had brought it with him or composed it in France. *"Anime voi..."* has survived in at least 17 different manuscript sources, showing that many musicians admired it and were willing to pay to have copies made.

Three different copyists wrote the three sources used for this edition, and there are considerable differences between them. Inasmuch as Rossi may have written different versions himself, we do not have a single "original" version. The choices made here have worked well in performance.

Sources

(1) No. 1 in a manuscript collection entitled *Cantate di Rossi e Savioni*, II 3947, F. 2422, Brussels, call number. This major source contains 35 cantatas, including *"Dimmi, amor"* by Arcangelo Lori (included in *Italian Arias of the Baroque and Classical Eras* (Alfred Publishing Co., 1994).

(2) No. 3 in a manuscript collection, G885, Rome. This leather bound volume, stamped with a gold crest of sun and eagle, contains 25 works, including cantatas by Carlo Caproli, Giacomo Carissimi, and Savioni.

(3) No. 12 in a manuscript collection, Chigi Q.VII.99, Vatican (re-printed in *Italian Cantata in the Seventeenth Century*, vol. 1. New York: Garland, 1986). A parchment bound, exceptionally clear manuscript, containing 13 works. Composer's name: Luige Rossi.

Additional manuscripts were also examined at the Vatican and at the Biblioteca Casanatense, Rome.

All sources are for voice (soprano clef) and continuo. Key: C minor with a signature of one flat.

Anime voi

Poet unknown

Luigi Rossi
Realization by John Glenn Paton
(Range: C4–G5)

A - ni - me voi,___ che se - te dal - le fu - rie d'a-bis - so op-pres-se o-

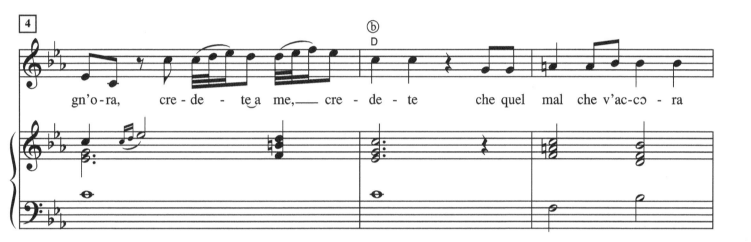

gn'o - ra, cre - de - te a me,___ cre - de - te che quel mal che v'ac-cɔ - ra

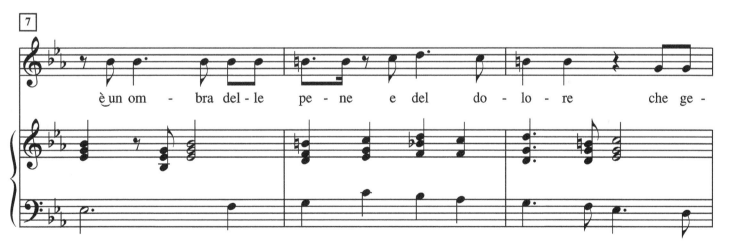

è un om - bra del - le pe - ne e del do - lo - re che ge-

ⓐ Recitatives are sung in a flexible tempo, following the emotions of the words. Relative note values should, however, be observed. In playing recitatives, the keyboard player may take many liberties, depending on the needs of the singer, the character of the instrument, and the acoustics of the room. Chords may be arpeggiated, enhanced or repeated, and bass notes may be doubled an octave below.

ⓑ *Appoggiaturas*: Stressed syllables are often sung one step higher than written, producing expressive dissonances. This occurs when there are two equal notes on the same pitch and the first one is stressed. Where an appoggiatura is recommended in this edition, the pitch named above the staff is to be sung instead of the printed note. Where two pitch names are given, such as "d-c", divide the printed note into two notes of equal length.

Translation: You souls who are constantly harried by the Furies of Hell, believe me: the evil that is afflicting you is only a suggestion of the pains and sorrow that

ⓒ Suggested tempo: ♩ = 84 – 92. All three of the source manuscripts contain the rising eighth notes given here in the right hand. In this period it is very unusual to find accompaniment notes other than bass notes.

a jealous lover feels. Whoever does not know what jealous is, could learn it from me. Let him ask my soul; he will learn it from my faithfulness.

man-di al-l'al - ma mi - a, lo sa - prà dal - la ___ mi - a fé, che di -

ran - no ch'un af - fan - no, un tor - men - to, un cruc - cio e-tɛ - rno, un

pur - ga - to-rio al-fin pɛg - gio è d'in-fɛr - no, che di-ran-no ch'un af -

fan - no, un tor - men-to, un cruc - cio e - te - rno, un pur - ga - to - rio al-

ⓓ In the middle of this bar, all three sources have a repeat bar (a single bar line with pairs of dots on both sides of it), suggesting a major sectional division.

They will say: an anxiety, a torment, an eternal worry, a Purgatory worse than Hell.

36

fin peg - gioè d'in - fer - no,____ Ta-le ap-pun-to lo

40

prɔ - vo ch'i-do-la - tran-do u-na bel-tà di - vi - na io tɛ-mo ch'o-gni

43

sguar - do d'a-man-te in-si-dia - tor non sia ra-pa - ce per

45

in - vo - lar quel bɛl che sì mi pia - ce. M'in-ge-lo-si - ce u-n'a-stro, mi tur-ba o-gni pia-

ⓔ Flexible tempo, following the emotions of the text.

That is just what I experience since loving a divine beauty. I fear that every sneaky lover may be plotting to take her away whom I love so much. Every star makes me jealous, every planet upsets me: I fear that

ⓕ Each manuscript source shows this transition in a different way. Source 1) has three beats in m53 with *"-ri"* on a half note and *"Di chi-"* on two eighth notes. The other sources show *"Di"* on a quarter note, but disagree on barring. I decided to keep that rhythm, but added the rests at the beginning of m54 to simplify the counting.

Heaven itself, being in love, could take away the beauty that has wounded me. Monstrous imaginings have stunned my mind; my heart is full of pains and spasms; I live

spa - smi;   sta fra cruc - ci la mia vi - ta.   O -

gn'om - bra m'a - dom - bra, il cɔ - re m'ab - ba - glia, ne mai da me sgom - bra sí

fiɛ - ra bat - ta - glia.   On - de ch'in - tor - men - tar - mi   for -

s'è   ch'io di - ca al - fin' in fiɔ - chi__ car -

ⓖ Suggested tempo: ♩. = 88 - 96   ⓗ Flexible tempo.

among worries. Every shadow makes me suspicious, my heart deceives me, and the battle never ends.
Therefore, perhaps tormenting myself, I say finally, in feeble poems:

(i) The repetition that begins here is indicated, but not written out, in sources 1) and 2). I believe that the repeated section should be only 12 measures long, but source (3) repeats 22 measures, through *"d'Inferno."*

Whoever does not know..., etc.

Fugga Amor / Segua Amor

/fuːgːga fuːgːgamoːr seːgwa seːgwamoːr/

Flee from Cupid / Follow Cupid

Mario Savioni (1608–1685)

/maːrjo savjoːni/

fuːgːga	fuːgːgamoːr		seːgwa	seːgwamoːr	ki	desiːa
1. Fugga,	**fugg'Amor**	/	**Segua,**	**segu'Amor**	**chi**	**desia**
Flee,	flee-from-Cupid,	/	Follow,	follow-Cupid,	whoever	desires

ke	feliːtʃe nel	sen	laːnima siːa
2. Che	**felice nel**	**sen**	**l'anima sia.**
that	happy in-the	bosom	the-soul may-be.

soːno i	prɛːmi	damoːre
3. Sono i	**premi**	**d'Amore**
Are the	rewards	of-Cupid,

doːpo	luŋgo servir	pɛːna e	doloːre
4. Dopo	**lungo servir**	**pena e**	**dolore.**
after	long serving,	pain and	sorrow.

5. Sono i premi d'Amore

doːpo	luŋgo servir	feːdet	amoːre
6. Dopo	**lungo servir**	**fede et**	**amore.**
...after	long serving,	faithfulness and	love.

non	segwiːte non	fudːdʒiːte	swɔi straːli
7. Non	**seguite / Non**	**fuggite**	**suoi strali!**
Do-not	follow / Do-not	flee-from	his arrows!

fanːno larmi	damoːr	pjaːge	mortaːli	vitaːli
8. Fanno l'armi	**d'Amor**	**piaghe**	**mortali. /**	**vitali.**
Make the-weapons	of-Cupid	wounds	fatal. /	vital.

Poetic Background

"Love will make you miserable." "Love will make you happy." It's all in your point of view.

Line 1: *Amore*, spoken of here as a person, is capitalized and his name is translated as Cupid.

Musical Background

Mario Savioni, who spent his whole long life in Rome, was a busy singer and composer. He sang his first opera role at the age of 11 or 12 and sang in important Roman church choirs, first as a soprano and later as an alto. In 1642 he sang in an opera by Luigi Rossi. He is thought to have been one of the musicians who served Queen Christina of Sweden, one of the most discerning patrons of music. At her court, as an old man, he may have known the young Alessandro Scarlatti.

This duet comes from a beautiful manuscript volume in the Vatican Library. It is bound on the narrow side and measures 4 inches (10cm) high by 10? inches (26.3 cm) wide, which was a normal format in the 1600s. On 100 parchment leaves a single copyist wrote 20 cantatas for solo soprano, three duets and a trio. At least four of the pieces were composed by "Luigi" (Rossi) and seven by "Mario" (Savioni). The composer of *"Fugga Amor"* is identified not in this source but in another manuscript in Bologna, according to a catalogue compiled by Irving Eisley.

The first tempo is not marked, but the later tempo markings are in the original manuscript.

Source

Manuscript Barb. lat. 4163, Vatican. For two voices (soprano clef) and continuo. Original key: A major with no key signature.

Fugga Amor / Segua Amor

Poet unknown

Mario Savioni
Realization by John Glenn Paton
[Range indicators: E4–F♯5 and E4 to G5]

@ Suggested tempo: ♩ = 124–136.

ⓑ Suggested tempo: ♩ = 92–100. Probably the first tempo should return in m14 although it is not marked.

Translation: (First voice:) Flee from love if you want to have peace in your soul. Love's rewards,
　　　　　　(Second voice:) Follow love if you want to have peace in your soul.

(First voice:) after long service, are pain and sorrow.
(Second voice:) Love's rewards, after long service, are faithfulness and love.

So - no i pre - mi d'A - mo - re   do - po lun - go ser -

re.   So - no i pre - mi d'A - mo - re   do - po lun - go ser -

vir   pe - na   e   do - lo   -   re.___

vir   fe - de   et__ a - mo -

So - no i pre - mi d'A - mo - re   pe - na e do - lo -

re.   So - no i pre - mi d'A - mo - re   do - po

re, do - po lun -

lun - go ser - vir fe - de et a - mo -

go ser - vir pe - na e do - lo -

re, fe - de

re._____ Non se - gui - te suoi

et a - mo - re.

Ⓒ **Presto** ⒟

ⓒ The original manuscript has repeat bars here to indicate that each half of the cantata should be sung twice.

ⓓ Suggested tempo: ♩. = 66–72.

(First voice:) Do not seek out his

ⓔ Like the previous adagio: ♩ = 92–100.

(First voice:) arrows. Love's weapons make deadly wounds.
(Second voice:) Follow his arrows.

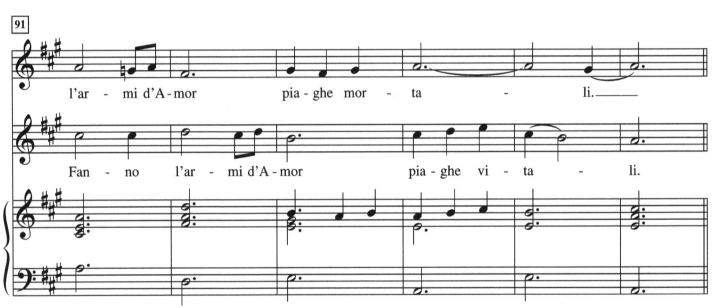

ⓕ Like the previous presto: ♩ = 66–72.

(Second voice:) Love's weapons make wounds of life.

Alfin m'ucciderete

/alfin mutːtʃidereːte/

At Last You Will Kill Me

Alessandro Scarlatti (1660–1725)

/alesːsandro skarlatːti/

First Recitative

alfin   mutːtʃidereːte o mjɛi pensjɛːri
1. **Alfin m'ucciderete,   o miei pensieri!**
At-last me-you-will-kill, oh my   thoughts!

da   me lontaːna ɛ klɔːri liːdolo miːo
2. **Da   me lontana è Clori, l'idolo mio.**
From me distant   is Clori, the-idol mine.

si ramːmentasːse   o dio
3. **Si rammentasse,   o Dio,**
If she-would-remember, o God,

de mjɛi kostanti amoːri
4. **De' miei costanti amori**
of my   faithful love

kon un sospiːro almeːno
5. **Con un sospiro almeno,**
with a sigh   at-least,

fiʎːʎo   del suo bɛl   seːno
6. **Figlio   del suo bel   seno!**
offspring of her beautiful bosom,

siŋkontrasːsero almeːno i   sospir mjɛːi
7. **S'incontrassero almeno i   sospir miei!**
If-met   at-least the sighs mine!

a me ke pɛnsaː   lɛːi
8. **A me che pensa a   lei,**
On me that thinks about her,

e tante vɔlteː   tante
9. **E   tante   volte e tante,**
and so-many times and so-many,

o se klɔːri pensasːse iŋ kwestistante
10. **O se Clori pensasse   in quest'istante!**
o, if Clori would-think at this-moment!

ma kisːsa   forse adːdɛsːso
11. **Ma chi sa?   Forse addesso**
But who knows? Maybe now

radʒoːna   kon altruːi
12. **Ragiona   con altrui**
she-is-conversing with someone-else,

ed in un punto istesːso
13. **Ed in un punto istesso**
And at a   point same

ei ferma il gwardo inelːla edelːla in luːi
14. **Ei ferma il guardo in ella ed ella in lui.**
he stops the gaze   on her and she on him.

e ki sa   ka   kwestoːra
15. **E   chi sa   ch'a quest'ora,**
And who knows but-at this hour,

dʒa   skordaːta di me non laːmi   aŋkoːra
16. **Già   scordata di me, non l'ami   ancora?**
already forgetful of me, not him-she-may-love yet?

lundʒi   dalːla mia mente
17. **Lungi   dalla mia mente,**
Far-away from my mind,

tiranːni del mio kɔr lundʒi volaːte
18. **Tiranni del mio cor, lungi   volate!**
tyrants of my heart, far-away fly!

se voi mi tormentaːte
19. **Se voi mi tormentate**
If you me torment

kon sospɛtːti si fjɛːri
20. **Con sospetti   si fieri,**
with suspicions so cruel,

21. **Alfin m'ucciderete, o miei pensieri!**

First Aria

io moriːrɛi kontɛnto
22. **Io morirei   contento**
I would-die happy

per non penar koziː
23. **Per non penar   così.**
so-as not to-suffer thus.

ma sol peruɲ momɛnto
24. **Ma sol per un momento**
But just for one moment

io rivedɛr   vorːrɛːi
25. **Io riveder   vorrei**
I again-to-see would-like

kolɛi ke tɔlse prija
26. **Colei che tolse pria**
her who took first

la paːtʃe‿alːlalma mija
27. **La pace all'alma mia**
the peace from-the-soul mine

e pɔi da me parti
28. **E poi da me partì.**
and then from me departed.

Second Recitative
klɔːri miːa klɔːri bɛlːla
29. **Clori mia, Clori bella,**
Clori mine, Clori beautiful,

aːi kwante vɔlte ai kwante
30. **Ahi, quante volte, ahi quante**
Alas, how-many times, alas, how-many,

ti vɔ tʃerkando in kwɛsta parte e‿in kwelːla
31. **Ti vo cercando in questa parte, e in quella,**
you I-go seeking in this place and in that

in kui lanimaːmante
32. **In cui l'anima amante**
in which the-spirit loving

trovaɾ solea bɛn spesːso
33. **Trovar solea ben spesso**
to-find was-accusomed very often

te ke sospiːɾa e non ritrɔːvaːdesːso
34. **Te che sospira, e non ritrova adesso.**
you, whom it-sighs-for, and not finds now.

peːna ke‿in lontananza
35. **Pena, che in lontananza**
Pain, that in distance

oɲːɲaltra peːnaːvantsa
36. **Ogn'altra pena avanza,**
every-other pain surpasses,

sai kwalɛ klɔːri miːa
37. **Sai qual è Clori mia?**
do-you-know what is Clori mine?

dɔːve del mio gran fɔːko
38. **Dove del mio gran foco**
Where of my great fire

ti ridiceaʎːʎardoːɾi
39. **Ti ridicea gl'ardori**
to-you were-spoken-again the-passions

vedeɾilːloːko e non vedervi klɔːɾi
40. **Veder il loco, e non vedervi, Clori?**
to-see the place and not to-see-you, Clori?

kwando pɔi dʒuŋgon loːre
41. **Quando poi giungon l'ore**
When, then, approach the-hours

ke per konfɔrto mio per mio kostuːme
42. **Che per conforto mio, per mio costume,**
that for comfort mine, for my custom,

venja del tuo bɛlːluːme
43. **Venìa del tuo bel lume**
came of your beautiful eye

lamaːto‿a vagedːdzar dolt ʃe splendoːɾe
44. **L'amato a vagheggiar dolce splendore,**
the-beloved to gaze-delightedly-at sweet splendor

per mia barbaɾa sɔrte
45. **Per mia barbara sorte,**
through my cruel fate

kwando dʒuŋgon kwelːloːɾe io dʒuŋgaːa mɔrte
46. **Quando giungon quell'ore, io giunga a morte,**
when approach those-hours, I approach to death,

onde kon insofːfriːbile martɔːɾo
47. **Onde, con insoffribile martoro,**
whereupon, with insufferable martyrdom

inuːnistɛsːso diː pju vɔlte io mɔːɾo
48. **In un istesso dì più volte io moro.**
in one single day more times I die.

Second Aria
faɾia la peːna miːa pjandʒerɛ i sasːsi
49. **Faría la pena mia piangere i sassi.**
Would-make the pain mine weep the stones.

i mɛsti sospir mjɛːi
50. **I mesti sospir miei**
The sad sighs mine

vɛŋgono dɔːve sɛi
51. **Vengono dove sei,**
come where you-are,

e se li sai sentiɾ
52. **E se li sai sentir,**
and if them you-can hear,

maskolteɾai laŋgwir dɔːve tu pasːsi
53. **M'ascolterai languir dove tu passi.**
me-you-will-listen-to languish where you pass.

Poetic Background

(Recitative) "O thoughts, you are torturing me as I imagine reasons to be jealous!" (Aria) "I would die happy if it would mean having no more jealousy—but I would like once more to see the one who made me so unhappy." (Recitative) "I look for you again and again, just as I used to do, but never find you." (Aria) "My misery would make even rocks sorry for me. If you listen, you will hear my sighs wherever you go."

Line 2: *Clori* is the name of a shepherdess in poems by Theocritus. (See more information in the notes to *"Amarilli, mia bella."*)

Line 18: *Tiranni* are the lover's jealous thoughts, which oppress him cruelly.

Line 26: *tolse* comes from *togliere. Pria* is a short form of *prima*.

Lines 43–44: *...Venía...splendore...*, is a distorted word order. Normal word order: *[Quando] l'amato venía per vagheggiare il splendore del tuo lume.* Translation: [When] the lover [the singer] came to admire the splendor of your eye...

Musical Background

This is the first modern edition of this masterpiece of the cantata repertoire. If one cantata is chosen to represent the prolific Scarlatti, *Alfin m'ucciderete* stands out from among the more than 780 others. It survives in more manuscripts than any other, at least 36, meaning that a remarkable number of performers and admirers copied it by hand or paid a professional copyist to do so. Also, Scarlatti chose this score, not one of his masses or operas, to place on the music rack beside him when he posed for an anonymous artist to paint his portrait (reproduced in *26 Italian Songs and Arias*, Alfred Publishing Co.).

Beyond such distinctions, this cantata stands out for its musical beauty and remarkable emotional intensity. The recitatives allow the singer to express varying shades of anxiety, mounting anger, despair and resignation. The first, moderately quick aria portrays the lover's anguish with many dissonant suspensions and with long, intricate melismas on the word *penar* (to suffer pain). In m68 there is a unique structural feature: the *seconda parte* seems to end and the *prima parte* begins again in the bass as expected, but the voice resumes singing for another two measures, forcing the *seconda parte* to cadence again in m70. The listener hears this delayed cadence as an intensification of the mood. The final, slower aria is in a *siciliano* rhythm that often expresses melancholy; the voice sings long dissonant notes over changing harmonies.

Scarlatti dated *Alfin m'ucciderete* on July 20, 1705. He was working in Rome, supplying cantatas and oratorios for concerts in the palaces of Cardinals Ottoboni and Pamphili. The opera theaters were all closed, as they often were during the reigns of unsympathetic popes.

Sources

(1) a modern copy, which Prof. Edwin Hanley of the University of California at Los Angeles allowed me to photocopy in 1978. It is a clear and accurate score, but unfortunately, the period source is unidentified.

(2) No. 18 in *Cantate diverse, Roma, 1722*, Regensburg. This source, containing only works of Scarlatti, is not listed in Prof. Hanley's catalog.

(3) No. 1 in Add. Ms. 31508, London (reprinted as no. 18 in *Italian Cantata in the Seventeenth Century*, vol. 13, ed. Malcolm Boyd, New York: Garland, 1986. M57-m62 are missing from the reprint.).

(4) No. 3 in *6 Cantate del Scarlatti*, Fond Kiesewetter SA.67.G.104, Vienna. R. G. Kiesewetter (1773–1850) made the copy and realized the harmonization, often doubling the voice part in the piano. The rhythmic figure in m57-m64 is borrowed from his version.

All sources are for voice (soprano clef) and continuo. Original key: G minor.

Alfin m'ucciderete

Poet unknonw

Alessandro Scarlatti
Realization by John Glenn Paton
(Range: D4–G5)

Al - fin,   al - fin m'uc-ci - de - re - te,   al - fin m'uc-ci - de - re - te,   o

miei pen - sie - ri!   Da me lon - ta - na è Clo - ri,   Clo - ri, l'i - do - lo

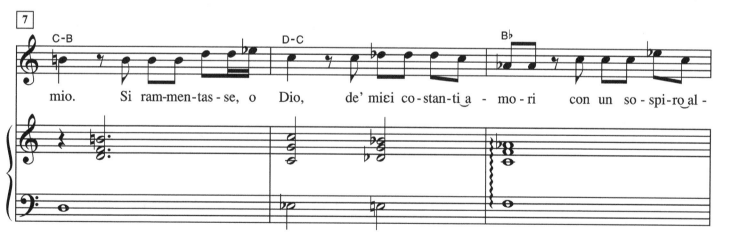

mio.   Si ram-men-tas - se, o Dio,   de' miei co - stan - ti a - mo - ri   con un so - spi - ro al -

ⓐ Recitatives are sung in a flexible tempo, following the emotions of the words. Relative note values should, however, be observed.

ⓑ *Appoggiaturas:* Stressed syllables are often sung one step higher than written, producing expressive dissonances. This occurs when there are two equal notes on the same pitch and the first one is stressed. Where an appoggiatura is recommended in this edition, the pitch named above the staff is to be sung instead of the printed note. Where two pitch names are given, such as "d-c", divide the printed note into two notes of equal length.

ⓒ At cadences, for instance here and in m24, the voice part sometimes clashes against the cadential chords. To avoid this, the instruments should wait while the singer cadences and play the chords after the singer has finished. As a result, the measure has five beats instead of four, an acceptable irregularity in a recitative. Such cases are given here with a broken line to indicate that the instruments play the cadence after the voice finishes.

Translation: Finally, you are going to kill me, o my thoughts! Clori, my idol, is far away from me. If only she would think about my faithful love with at least a sigh,

10

Bb   C   Ab   Bb–Ab

me - no, fi - glio del suo bel se - no! S'in-con-tras-se - ro al - me-no   i so-spir miɛi!   A

13

Bb–A   D '

me,   a me che pen-sa a lɛi, e tan-te vol-te e tan-te, ɔ———— se Clɔ - ri pen-

16

Ab

sas - se   in   que - st'i - stan - te!   Ma chi sa, chi

ⓓ

18

C–D   F

sa? For-se a-dɛs - so   ra - gio-na con al-trui   ed in un pun-to i-stes - so   ei

ⓓ When the bass part is written in long notes, it may be effective to play them as short notes, leaving the singer momentarily unaccompanied (for instance, in measures 17–21 and 98–100).

the offspring of her beautiful bosom! If only my sighs would reach her! If only Clori would think at this instant of me, who thinks of her so many, many times! But who knows? Perhaps right now she is talking to another man and at the same moment

fer-ma il guar-do in el-la ed el-la in lu - i. E chi sa ch'a que - st'o - ra, già scor-da - ta di

me, non l'a-mi an-co - ra? Lun-gi, lun - gi dal-la mia men-te, ti - ran - ni del mio

cor, lun - gi vo-la - te! Se voi mi tor-men-ta - te con so-spɛt - ti si fiɛ - ri, al -

fin m'uc-ci - de - re - te, al - fin m'uc-ci - de - re - te, o miɛi pen-siɛ - ri!

each one gazes at the other. And who knows if at this moment, forgetting me, she is not falling in love with him?
Get far away from my mind, tyrants of my heart, fly far away! Finally, you are going to kill me, o my thoughts!

ⓔ "At an appropriate tempo." Suggested tempo: ♩ = 76–84.

I would die happy, not suffering like this.

But just for a moment I would like to see again the woman who first stole my peace and then left me.

Ma sol___ per un mo-men - to io ri-ve-der vor-rε - i co-lεi___ che tol-se pria

la pa - ce al-l'al - ma mia   e pɔi,   e pɔi   da me par - tì,___

e pɔi   da___ me___ par - tì,___   par - tì,

D.S. al Fine

par - tì,   da me par - tì.

Clori mine, beautiful Clori, alas, how many times I look for you in one place and in another where my loving soul often used to find you for whom I sigh and whom I no longer find. Pain that far surpasses any other pain—Clori,

do you know what it is like? To see the place where I told you about the great longing in my heart, and not see you, Clori? Then, when the hours approach when, to comfort myself, it was my habit to come to admire the beloved sweet splendor of your eyes, through my cruel fate, when those hours draw near, I draw near to death.

96

l'o - re,   io giun-ga a mor - te,   on-de,   con in-sof - fri - bi-le mar-to - ro,   in

99

un i - stes - so dì   più vol - te,   più vol - te io mo - ro.

102 Aria ⓕ

104

Fa - ría   la pe - na

ⓕ Suggested tempo: ♪. = 56–62. This tempo is called *"siciliano."*

Therefore, with insufferable martyrdom, in one single day I die many times. My pain would make stones weep.

ría la pe - na mi - a———— pian - ge-re i sas -

si,— pian - ge-re, pian - ge-re i sas - si,

pian - ge-re, pian - ge-re i sas - si,

pian-ge-re i sas - si.   I mɛ-sti so - spir miɛ - i

My sad sighs

come to where you are, and if you know how to hear them, you will listen to me languishing where you pass by.

Dopo tante e tante pene

/doːpo tˈanteː tˈante pɛːne/
After So Much Pain

Francesco Bartolomeo Conti (1681–1732)
/frantˈʃesko bartolomˈeːo kˈonti/

First aria:

doːpo tˈanteː   tˈante   pˈeːne
1. **Dopo tante e tante   pene**
   After so-many and so-many pains

duːna krˈuːda lontanˈantsa
2. **D'una cruda lontananza,**
   of-a cruel   distant-separation,

pˈuːrˈe alfˈin a vˈoi ritˈorno
3. **Pure alfin a voi ritorno,**
   then at-last to you I-return,

vˈaːge lˈuːtʃe del mˈiːo bɛn
4. **Vaghe luci   del mio ben.**
   lovely lights of my good.

sɛnto dʒaː   ke pju serˈeːne
5. **Sento già   che più serene**
   I-feel already that more serenely

spiːran lˈaure   in si bɛl   dʒˈorno
6. **Spiran l'aure   in sì bel   giorno,**
   blow   the-breezes in such beautiful day,

e   ritˈorna la sperˈantsa
7. **E   ritorna la speranza**
   and returns —hope

a brilːlˈar dˈɛntro il mˈio sen
8. **A brillar dentro il mio sen.**
   to sparkle in   — my bosom.

Recitative:

dubˈːbjo di   vˈɔstra fˈeːde
9. **Dubbio di   vostra fede,**
   Doubt   about your faithfulness,

kwˈantoː   dˈio tormentˈɔː lˈaːnima mˈiːa
10. **Quanto, o   Dio, tormentò l'anima mia.**
    as-much-as, oh God, tormented the-soul mine.

tirˈanːna dʒelozˈiːa non spɛnse   nˈɔ
11. **Tiranna gelosia   non spense,   nò,**
    tyrannical jealousy not extinguished, no,

makkrˈɛbːbe il mˈio bɛl   fˈɔːko
12. **Ma accrebbe il mio bel   foco,**
    but increased — my beautiful fire,

ke   per   fjɛːro destˈiːno
13. **Che per   fiero destino,**
    which through harsh destiny

o   lontˈaːno o vitʃˈiːno
14. **O   lontano o vicino**
    whether far   or near

kɛsːser pɔsːsiːo sɛntsa kandʒar mˈai tˈempre
15. **Ch'esser poss'io, senza cangiar mai tempre,**
    to-be   I-am-able, without changing ever natural-disposition

per vˈoi kˈare pupilːleˈ ardeːraː   sˈempre
16. **Per voi, care pupille, arderà   sempre!**
    for you, dear eyes,   it-will-burn always!

Second Aria:

kwˈelːla fjˈamːma ke   matˈːtʃɛnde
17. **Quella fiamma   che   m'accende**
    That   flame   which me-kindles

pjaːtʃe tˈanto alˈːlalma   mˈiːa
18. **Piace tanto   all'alma   mia**
    pleases so-much to-the-soul mine

ke   dʒamˈːmai sestingwerˈaː
19. **Che giammai   s'estinguerà!**
    that never   itself-will-it-extinguish.

e   se il fˈaːto a vˈoi mi rˈɛnde
20. **E   se il fato a voi mi rende,**
    And if— fate   to you me returns,

vˈaːgi rˈaːi del mˈiːo bɛl   sˈoːle
21. **Vaghi rai del mio bel   sole,**
    Lovely rays of my   beautiful sun,

ˈaltra lˈuːtʃelˈːla non vwˈɔːle
22. **Altra luce ella   non vuole**
    other light it   not wants

ne volˈer dʒamˈːmai potrˈaː
23. **Né voler   giammai potrà.**
    nor to-wish ever   will-it-be-able.

Poetic Background

(Aria) "For a long time we were separated, but now we are together again and I am happy." (Recitative) "My doubts and jealousy tormented me, but made me realize that I shall love you forever." (Aria) "My love for you brings me such happiness that it will never end, and if you become mine, I shall never want any other love."

Lines 11–16: *Tiranna...sempre* is all one sentence that is constructed with characteristically Baroque complexity. Its essential elements are: "Jealousy... increased my fire (passion), which... will burn forever."

Musical Background

This cantata is important because of the great popularity of its second aria, *"Quella fiamma..."*, widely, but falsely known as a work of Benedetto Marcello. Personal letters to this editor certify: that the cantata is not Marcello's, according to Dr. Eleanor Selfridge-Field, who catalogued all of Marcello's works; and that it is a genuine composition of Conti, according to Dr. Hermine W. Williams, the leading authority on Conti.

A. G. Ritter used a source that is not known to us when he published *Dopo tante e tante pene* as a work of Marcello's in a series entitled *Armonia* (Magdeburg: Hinrichshofen, ca. 1870). Ritter's transcribed the vocal line and text accurately, but in writing the piano part he sometimes took melodies from the basso continuo and put them into the right hand of the piano.

Carl Banck excerpted the second aria, *"Quella fiamma,"* in *Arien und Gesänge älterer Tonmeister* (Leipzig: Kistner, ca. 1880) to create his own fantastic version. He took words from the preceding recitative, beginning with *"Il mio bel foco,"* and used them to construct a brief recitative in a Romantic style. He gave the aria a tempo of *allegretto affettuoso*, an extravagantly pianistic accompaniment, and an outlandish vocal cadenza. Banck's version was re-published by Alessandro Parisotti in *Arie antiche*, Vol. 1 (Milan: Ricordi, 1885) and it is still in print with various publishers in spite of its distortions.

Ferdinand Sieber copied Ritter's version of the complete cantata in the series *Caecilia* (Offenbach: André, ca. 1886, and still in print in Germany). Sieber added dynamics, phrasings and a tempo of *Andante sostenuto* for the second aria.

In this edition the correct composer's name and the authentic basso continuo part are printed for the first time. This version of *"Quella fiamma..."* was sung for the first time by tenor Yasushi Shiba in Tokyo in 2002.

Source

No. 13 in a manuscript collection, pp. 65-68, Mus. ms. 30.226, Berlin. For voice (soprano clef) and continuo. Key: C minor with two flats.

The same library also has a completely different, anonymous composition of the text *Dopo tante e tante pene*, for soprano, violin and continuo (Mus. ms. 30339).

Dopo tante e tante pene

Francesco Bartolomeo Conti
Realization by John Glenn Paton
(Range: D4–G5)

Poet unknown

(Do - po tan - te e tan - te pe - ne d'u - na cru - da lon - ta -
nan - za, pu - re al - fin a voi ri - tor - no, va - ghe lu - ci __ del mio ben. Do - po
tan - te e tan - te pe - ne, pu - re al - fin a voi ri - tor - no, va - ghe lu - ci __ del mio
ben. pu - re al - fin a voi ri - tor - no, va - ghe lu - ci __ del mio bɛn.)

ⓐ Suggested tempo: ♩ = 48 – 54.

ⓑ In the original manuscript the *da capo* repetition is not written out. It is printed here to offer suggestions about ornamentation as well as variations in the accompaniment. Where double notes are printed, the singer must choose which to sing. Like all ornamentations, these are optional and the singer may feel free to ignore them or to invent others in an appropriate style.

Translation: After so many, many pains of a cruel separation, now at last I return to you, o lovely eyes of my beloved.

Already I feel that warm breezes blow more gently on such a beautiful day, and hope sparkles again in my heart.

Do - po tan - te e tan - te pe — ne d'u - na cru - da lon - ta -

nan - za, pu - re al-fin a voi ri-tor - no, va - ghe lu - ci del mio bɛn. Do - po

tan - te e tan - te pe — fin a voi ri-tor - no, va - ghe lu - ci del mio

bɛn. pu - re al-fin a voi ri-tor - no, va - ghe lu - ci del mio bɛn.

ⓒ Flexible tempo, observing relative note values.

ⓓ *Appoggiaturas*: Stressed syllables are often sung one step higher than written, producing expressive dissonances. This occurs when there are two equal notes on the same pitch and the first one is stressed. Where an appoggiatura is recommended in this edition, the pitch named above the staff is to be sung instead of the printed note. Where two pitch names are given, such as "d-c", divide the printed note into two notes of equal length.

(Recitative) Doubt about your faithfulness—O God, how much it tormented my soul! Tyrannical jealousy did not extinguish, no, it increased my flaming desire, and it is my destiny that whether I am far away or

ci - no ch'esser poss'io, sen - za can - giar mai tem - pre, per

voi, ca - re pu - pil - le ar - de - rà sem - pre!

Quel - la_____ fiam - ma_____ che m'ac - cen - de

ⓔ Suggested tempo: ♪ = 124 – 136.

near to you, without changing in the slightest, I will love you forever!
(Second aria) That flame which sets me on fire

makes my soul so happy that it will never be extinguished.

64
cen - de pia-ce tan-to al-l'al - ma___ mi - a che___ giam - mai s'e-stin-gue-

68
rà,___ s'e-stin - gue - rà,_____

72
___ s'e-stin-gue - rà, s'e-stin - gue - rà!

76
E   se il

And if

fate returns me to you, lovely rays of the beautiful sun, my soul does not desire any other light,
nor will it ever want any other.

giam-mai   po - tra.

Quel - la_____   fiam - ma_____   che m'ac - cen - de

ⓕ In the original manuscript the *da capo* repetition is not written out. It is printed here to offer suggestions about ornamentation as well as variations in the accompaniment.

112

Quel - la_____ fiam - ma_____ che___ m'ac -

116

cen - de pia - ce tan-to al-l'al-ma mi - a che giam-mai s'e-stin-gue -

120

rà,_____ che giam-mai s'e-stin-gue - rà,_____

123

_____ s'e-stin - gue - rà! Quel - la___ fiam - ma_ che m'ac-

cen - de pia - ce tan-to al-l'al - ma___ mi - a che___ giam - mai s'e-stin-gue -

rà,___ s'e-stin - gue - rà,_____

___ s'e-stin-gue - rà, s'e-stin - gue - rà!

Alfin m'ucciderete

/alfin mutːt ʃidereːte/

At Last You Will Kill Me

Francesco Durante (1684–1755)

/frantʃesko durante/

Note: The text of this duet is the same as the first recitative from the cantata by the same name by Alessandro Scarlatti. The phonetic transcription and word-by-word translation are found on page 000.

Musical Background

Duets were a favorite medium of chamber music throughout the Baroque era, used both for public performance and for voice teaching. After a singing student's vocal technique was established, a way of learning style and expression was to sing duets with the teacher. According to some sources, that is the purpose of Durante's *"12 Chamber Duets for Learning to Sing."* (Durante also composed *solfeggi*, wordless singing exercises, for learning to sing; two of them are found in *26 Italian Songs and Arias*, Alfred Publishing Co.)

Durante had the extraordinary idea of basing his duets on cantatas by Alessandro Scarlatti, who must have been an admired older friend. Even more surprisingly, most of the duets are not based on Scarlatti's melodious arias but on phrases taken from the introductory recitatives of the cantatas. *"Alfin m'ucciderete"* shows how Durante usually built his duets: the voices echo each other until an expressive phrase offers a chance for the voices to repeat and develop a more continuous musical texture.

Durante's duets were greatly admired for their ingenuity and beauty, and singing teachers must have considered them highly useful as well. They survive in at least 16 manuscript copies, one of them dated 1720. It seems that they were never published in Italy, but after 1800 the whole series was published in various editions in France, Germany and Russia. Knud Jeppesen published two of the duets in *La Flora* (Copenhagen: Wilhelm Hansen, 1949).

Most of Durante's duets were composed with conventional key signatures, but this one has none. It begins and ends in G minor but goes to far distant keys, just like Scarlatti's recitative.

The extended range of the soprano part is noteworthy; the soprano's high B was almost never used in the previous century. A passionately dramatic delivery will require that the singers agree on the dynamics that they want to use.

The primary source used here has a piano part realized from the basso continuo by Franciszek Mirecki (1791–1862), "reviewed and corrected" by Mirecki's teacher, Luigi Cherubini (1760–1842), the Italian-born Director of the Paris Conservatory. Mirecki apparently worked from a manuscript source without bass figures. A few changes have been made in his harmonization for the sake of consistency with the solo version earlier in this book.

Source

(1) No. 13 (sic) of *Duetti del Signor Durante* (Paris: Carli [between 1822–1828]), G.18.H.23, Rome. Two voices (soprano and alto clefs) and piano. Key: G minor, no key signature.

(2) No. 12 of *XII Duetti da Camera per imparar a cantare* (Leipzig: Breitkopf & Härtel [1844]), Regensburg. Continuo realized by F. Maier. Two voices (treble clefs) and piano. Key: G minor, no key signature.

Duet: Alfin m'ucciderete

Poet unknown

Francesco Durante
Adapted from the continuo realization by F. Mirecki
(Range: A3–E5 and E4–B5)

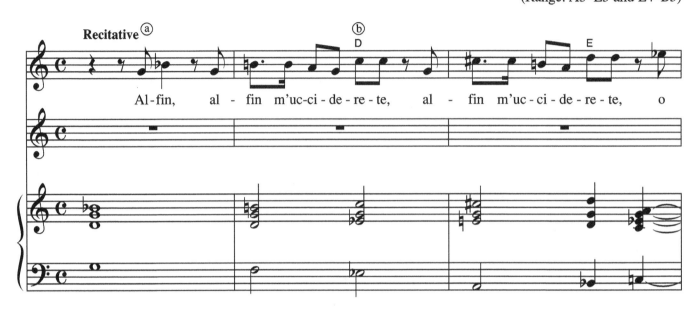

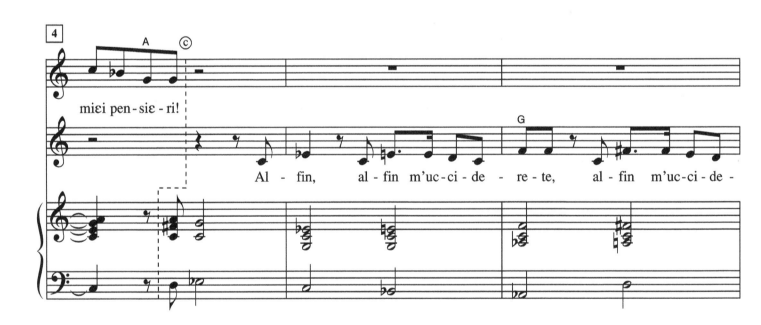

ⓐ Recitatives are sung in a flexible tempo, following the emotions of the words. Relative note values should, however, be observed. In playing recitatives, the keyboard player may take many liberties, depending on the needs of the singer, the character of the instrument, and the acoustics of the room. Chords may be arpeggiated, enhanced or repeated, and bass notes may be doubled an octave below.

ⓑ *Appoggiaturas:* Stressed syllables are often sung one step higher than written, producing expressive dissonances. This occurs when there are two equal notes on the same pitch and the first one is stressed. Where an appoggiatura is recommended in this edition, the pitch named above the staff is to be sung instead of the printed note. Where two pitch names are given, such as "d-c", divide the printed note into two notes of equal length.

ⓒ At cadences, for instance here and in m7, the voice part sometimes clashes against the cadential chords. To avoid this, the instruments should wait while the singer cadences and play the chords after the singer has finished. As a result, the measure has five beats instead of four, an acceptable irregularity in a recitative. Such cases are shown here with a broken line to indicate that the instruments play the cadence after the voice finishes.

Translation: In the end, you are going to kill me, o my thoughts!

ⓓ Both sources say *a tempo* here and in similar passages later. Only source (2) says *Andante*. Suggested tempo: ♩ = 72–80.

ⓔ The appoggiaturas, sung as two eighth-notes, are found only in source (1).

Clori, my idol, is far away from me. If only she would think about my faithful love with at least a sigh, the offspring of her beautiful bosom!

ⓕ When the bass part is written in long notes, it may be effective to play them as short notes, leaving the singer momentarily unaccompanied (for instance, in measures 20–24 and 28–36).

If only my sighs would reach her! If only Clori would think at this instant of me, who thinks of her so many, many times!

But who knows? Perhaps right now she is talking to another man and at the same moment each one gazes at the other.

And who knows if at this moment, forgetting me, she is not falling in love with him? Get far away from my mind, tyrants of my heart, fly far away!

In the end, you are going to kill me, o my thoughts!

Dite ch'ogni momento

/ˈdiːte koɲːˈɲi moˈmɛnto/

Say That Every moment

    ˈdiːte koɲːˈɲi   moˈmɛnto
1. **Dite ch'ogni momento**
    Say   that every moment

    ˈdɛsːsa ˈkjaːmo e   ramːˈmɛnto
2. **D'essa chiamo e   rammento,**
    of-her I-call   and remember,

    e   nel   pju ˈgraːve ˈdwɔːlo
3. **E   nel   più grave duolo**
    And in-the most serious sorrow

    nonˈɔː   per ˈmio konsˈwɔːlo
4. **Non ho   per mio consuolo**
    not I-have for my consolation

    kil   ˈsoːlo lagriˈmar
5. **Ch'il solo lagrimar.**
    but   only to-weep.

    e   se riˈpɔːzo ˈbraːma
6. **E   se riposo brama**
    And if repose she-wishes

    ˈdaːre a ˈmjɛi ˈluːmi inˈtanto
7. **Dare a miei lumi intanto,**
    to-give to my   eyes meanwhile,

    ˈtorni a   ki oɲːˈɲor la ˈkjaːma
8. **Torni   a   chi ognor la chiama,**
    may-she-return to him who her   — calls

    ed avˈraː   ˈtrɛːgwa il ˈpjanto
9. **Ed avrà   tregua il pianto,**
    and will-have respite   the weeping,

    ˈtɛrmine il sospiˈrar
10. **Termine il sospirar.**
    end   the sighing.

Poetic Background

The poet says to the passing breezes, "Say that I am longing for my lover to come back to me."

Lines 4-5: *non ho... ch'il*: the idiom *non...che* means "only." *Consuolo* is obsolete; modern Italian uses *consolazione*. *Il* is superfluous and is not translated.

Lines 9–10: *avrà* governs both lines: "weeping *will have* respite, sighing *will have* an end."

Giovanni Battista Pergolesi (1710–1736)
/dʒoˈvanːni batːˈtista pergoˈleːzi/

Musical Background

This aria is a novel experiment, probably unique in its period in using a fully written out keyboard part for the introduction. After the voice enters (m9), the keyboard part becomes a single line *basso continuo*, but the busy 16th notes are written in a style that is more idiomatic for the keyboard than the cello. Pergolesi knew, perhaps from hearing Domenico Scarlatti's innovative keyboard music, that a harpsichord could do much more than simply play block chords and double the cello part in a cantata. This aria anticipates the classical style, in which keyboard parts were fully written out and the piano gradually became an expressive partner to the singing voice.

In the complete cantata this aria is preceded by a recitative, *"Dalsigre, ahi Dalsigre,"* and followed by a second recitative and a second aria. The other movements are attractive but much more conventional.

The cantata is the first of four that were published within months after Pergolesi died at the age of 26. Gioacchino Bruno, contrabassist in the *Real Cappella* (royal orchestra) of Naples and probably a friend of Pergolesi's, assembled them for publication. The other three cantatas use stringed instruments in addition to the continuo.

Source (1) presents a rhythmic problem in m18, also in measures 19, 37 and 38. Each measure begins with eight 16th notes, but the last three are grouped into a triplet, making the measure one 16th note short. The solution chosen here, changing the first 16th to an eighth, is confirmed by the placement of the syllables; if the triplet were eliminated, the syllables would occur in an oddly syncopated way.

Another problem occurs in m35: on beat 1 the voice has a flatted note that is not flatted in m36, and there is no flat in the bass until the last note of m36. Figures below the bass indicate a minor chord on m35, beat 1, but major chords on m35, beat 3, and m36, beats 1 and 3. Source (2) interprets the entire passage in minor, but the changes of mode given here are also possible.

Source

(1) *Cantata I. Per Cembalo*, from *Quattro cantate da camera*, Opus 2 (Napoli: Palmiero, 1736?), Regensburg. (The composer's name is given as Giovan-Battista Pergolese.) Original Key: B-flat Major.

(2) *Opera omnia*, vol. 21, ed. F. Caffarelli (Rome: Gli amici della musica da camera, 1941). (Caffarelli worked from a manuscript in the British Library, and produced a highly edited version with added expression marks. This cantata is given the date 1732 and a title *Lontananza*, distance.) Key: B-flat Major.

Dite ch'ogni momento

Poet unknown

Giovanni Battista Pergolesi
Realization by John Glenn Paton
(Range: D4–G5)

ⓐ Suggested tempo: ♩ = 66-72

ⓑ Play the grace notes ahead of the beat (shorten the last note of m2).

ⓒ The trill begins on the printed note (other solutions are possible: [Musical example] JP: please write out all examples

ⓓ The trill in the alto voice may be played this way (other solutions are also possible): [Musical example]

Translation: Say that at every moment

ⓔ Sing the grace notes and the syllable *chia-* ahead of the beat by shortening the last note of m10. [Musical example]

ⓕ The trill may be sung this way (other solutions are possible): [Musical example]

ⓖ Lengthen the *appoggiatura*:][Musical example]

I call out for her and remember, and in very great sorrow my only consolation is in weeping.

ⓗ [Musical example]

duo - lo non __ ho __ per __ mi-o con - suo-lo   ch'il so - __ lo

la - gri - mar, ch'il so-lo __ la - gri - mar.

Di - te   che d'es - sa   chia - mo,   ram-men - to

o - gni mo-men-to,   e   nel   più   gra - ve

ⓘ Sing the syllable and the grace notes ahead of the beat, as in m11.

ⓙ [Musical example]

ⓚ The first edition has a *fermata* sign here rather than a *fine*. When this measure is played the first time, there is no stopping or slowing of the tempo. The second time, the keyboard part ends on beat 4 with a single note in the right hand, with or without a bass note. There may be a slight *ritardando* for the ending.

And if she wants to give peace again to my

lu - mi in-tan - to,   tor - ni a chi o - gnor   la

chia - ma,   tor - ni a chi o - gnor   la chia - ma,

ed   a - vrà tre - gua il   pian - to,   ter - mi - ne il

so - spi - rar,   ter - mi - ne il so - spi - rar.

Da Capo al Fine

① The trill may be sung this way (other solutions are possible): [Musical example]

ⓜ Lengthen the *appoggiatura*, as in m14, both here and in m48.

weeping eyes, may she return to one who calls her, and his sighing will come to an end.

Nò, non vedrete mai

nɔ non vedrɛːte maːi

My Love Will Not Change

nɔ non vedrɛːte maːi
1. **Nò, non vedrete mai**
No, not you-will-see ever

kandʒar ʎafːfɛtːti mjɛːi
2. **Cangiar gli affetti miei,**
to-change the affections mine,

bɛi luːmi ondɛ imparaːi
3. **Bei lumi, onde imparai**
Beautiful lights, where I-learned

a sospiɾaɾ damor
4. **A sospirar d'amor.**
to sigh from-love.

kwel kɔr ke vi donaːi
5. **Quel cor che vi donai**
That heart that to-you I-gave

pju kjɛːder non potrɛːi
6. **Più chieder non potrei**
again to-ask not I-could,

ne kjɛːder lo vorːrɛːi
7. **Ne chieder lo vorrei**
nor to-ask it I-would-want

se lo potɛsːsi aɲkor
8. **Se lo potessi ancor.**
if it I-could again.

Poetic Background

"No, I will never change my love. I would never ask you to give back the heart that I gave you."

When he was ten years old, Pietro Trapassi (1698–1782) attracted attention with his talent for improvising verses. A wealthy patron took over his education and changed his name to Metastasio, which meant the same thing as Trapassi (between steps) but sounded more elegant because it came from Greek roots. After writing successful opera librettos in Rome, Metastasio spent most of his life at the imperial court in Vienna. He became the most important librettist in history, admired both for the beauty of his language and the high moral quality of his dramas. Because there were no copyrights, Metastasio's works were re-printed dozens of times and composers often went to them to find texts for vocal music.

This poem comes from *Ciro riconosciuto* (Cyrus Recognized), a libretto that Metastasio wrote in Vienna in 1736. It was set to music by Antonio Caldara and subsequently by 24 other composers. The opera elaborates on a story from the ancient historian, Herodotus. A prophet told the King of Media that he would be overthrown by a descendant, and to prevent this he exiled his son and gave orders to kill his baby grandson, Cyrus. Contrary to orders, Cyrus was placed with a shepherd who raised him as his own son. In the opera Cyrus learns his true identity and then must prove his identity to others, including his parents, who have returned from exile. Ultimately, he wins his grandfather's throne.

Cyrus sings *"No, non vedrete mai"* to a woman who returned his love in spite of his lowly status as a shepherd. Learning that he is of royal blood, she fears that she is unworthy of him, but he reassures her that his feelings toward her have not changed.

Line 1: *mai* is sung in two syllables instead of one. Righini recognized that the poet intended each line of verse to be a *settenario,* a line of seven syllables. Lines 4 and 8 are also *settenari,* although the final syllable of each is truncated.

Line 3: *lumi* is a metaphor for the beloved's bright eyes.

Line 6: *chieder,* that is, "ask you to give back my heart."

Musical Background

After training in Bologna, Italy, Righini went north to the German-speaking areas to make a long and successful career. It was due to this that Righini became expert in the new Classical style years ahead of other Italian composers. He was using fully written out piano parts at a time when composers in Italy had still not realized the potential of the rapidly developing "fortepiano." His contemporaries considered that he combined a genuine Italian vocal style with German skill in form and instrumentation.

Righini was so respected in his time that after his death a Berlin publisher issued a series of compositions that he had left unpublished (the German word *Nachlass* means "what is left behind"). This is one of four Italian songs that make up third volume.

This song is no casual *canzonetta.* The apparent spontaneity and simple texture of the music conceal a subtle mastery of Classical form, as it had developed in the music of Haydn and Mozart.

The piano begins with a downward figure that will later appear several times in the voice part. The voice enters impetuously in the middle of m2, introducing a phrase of expressive recitative (a slight *ritenuto* is effective in m5, with *a tempo* in m6). The first part moves to the dominant key and ends with piano arpeggios that will also end the song. A formal second part seems to begin in m19, but the music already returns to the tonic key in m24. Surprisingly, the music of mm24-27 is a variation of the recitative that was heard in mm3-6. The cadential phrase from mm5-6 shows up several more times in an insistent, but continually varied coda. The *sforzati* in the piano postlude seem to show that Righini knew some of Beethoven's music, too. Righini expected considerable agility from the singer, especially in quick descending scales. Rhythmic independence is also required, as the voice, singing over triplets in the piano, may have 2, 3, 4, 6 or 8 notes in a beat

Source

V. Righini's Nachlass von Gesang Compositionen... Drittes Heft (Berlin: Schlesinger [1814]). This source was obtained through the generosity of Dr. Edwin

Penhorwood, the editor of Righini's *12 Ariette*, Opus 7 (San Antonio: Southern Music, 1992). Original Key: E-flat Major.

Nò, non vedrete mai

Pietro Metastasio

Vincenzo Righini
Edited by John Glenn Paton
(Range: D4–G5)

ⓐ "Walking or going lively." Suggested tempo: [quarter] = 80-88.

ⓑ Earlier composers would have shown this appoggiatura with a small note, but Righini used a full-sized note (see also m14), as later composers normally did. Righini's precise notation here implies that the singer should not spontaneously add appoggiaturas in other phrases, as one might do in earlier music.

  The grace note preceding beat 4 is an *appoggiatura breve*, or *acciaccatura*, because it precedes a group of even, quick notes. Its value is stolen from beat 3.

Translation: No, you will never see me change my affections, oh beautiful eyes that taught me to sigh for love.

mor, bei lu - mi, on-de_im-pa - ra - i a

so - spi - rar_ d'a - mor,_ a so - spi -

rar, a_ so - spi - rar d'a - mor.

Quel_

ⓒ Observe the rest that interrupts the word *sospirar*. This artistic representation of agitated sighing is one of the hallmarks of the Classical era. In the art of rhetoric, it is called by the Latin term *suspiratio*. Examples are found in arias by Mozart (e.g., "Smanie implacabili" from *Così fan tutte*) and in several later songs in this volume.

That

ⓓ This notation of a turn is unusual and is open to several interpretations. One of the simplest would be to sing the four grace notes on the second beat, replacing the dot of the dotted quarter. The end result, however, should be graceful and expressive, not mathematical.

ⓔ Sing the appoggiaturas as even eighth notes. (The source does not have a natural sign before beat 2, but it seems required.)

heart that I gave you—I could never ask to have it back again, nor would I want to even if I could.

lo po-tes - si_an - cor, ne___ chiɛ -der lo vor -

rɛ - i se lo po-tes - si_an - cor, ne___ chiɛ - der_ lo_ vor -

rɛ - i se lo po-tes - si_an - cor.

Già la notte s'avvicina

/dʒa la nɔtːte savːvitʃiːna/

Already the Night Draws Near

Isabella Colbran-Rossini (1785–1845)

[izabɛlːla kolbrạn rosːsiːni]

dʒa	la nɔtːte savːvitʃiːna		
1. Già	**la notte s'avvicina—**		
Already	the night draws-near		

vjɛːni o niːtʃe amaːto bɛːne			
2. Vieni, o Nice, amato bene,			
Come, o Nice, beloved good,			

delːla plaːtʃida mariːna		
3. Della placida marina		
of-the peaceful seaside		

le freskaure a respirạr		
4. Le fresch'aure a respirar.		
the fresh-breezes to breathe.		

non sa	dir	ke	siːa	dilɛtːto
5. Non sa	**dir**	**che**	**sia**	**diletto**
Not knows-how	to-say	what	may-be	delight

ki	non	pɔːzạ iɲ	kwɛste arɛːne	
6. Chi	**non**	**posa**	**in queste**	**arene**
one-who	does-not	rest	on these	sands

or	kun	lɛnto	dzefːfirɛtːto
7. Or	**ch'un**	**lento**	**zeffiretto**
now	that-a	slow	little-breeze

doltʃemɛnte iɲkrɛspạ il	mar		
8. Dolcemente	**increspa il**	**mar.**	
gently	ripples	the sea.	

Poetic Background

"Come with me to the seaside to enjoy the cool night air."

For information about the poet, read the commentary to the preceding song. Metastasio, the most successful opera librettist in history, also wrote many texts for cantatas. This poem is the first of two arias in a cantata, *La pesca* (Fishing). This and other cantata texts are said to have been inspired by Metastasio's relationship with a famous singer, Marianna Bulgarelli Benti (1684–1734).

Rossini used this poem for a duet for two sopranos in the group of songs called *Soirées musicales* (see another song from that group on page 000).

Line 2: *Nice* comes from the name of the goddess of victory, called Nike by the Greeks and Victoria by the Romans. The phrase *amato bene* is masculine, although it describes a woman.

Line 5: *sia*: One may give equal length to the two vowels, considering that the [i] is stressed on the high tone (but it must have at least the length of an eighth note.).

Musical Background

When the turbulence of the Napoleonic era ended, a new Italian middle class rose in prosperity and produced a large number of capable, enthusiastic amateur musicians. They enjoyed making music at home around the piano, taking advantage of cheaply available printed music that was produced with new, quickly evolving printing techniques. Fully notated piano parts made it possible for amateur pianists to play well without the knowledge of harmony that had been necessary to play from Baroque *continuo* parts.

Romanza was the most common general term for songs for voice and piano in the early 1800s. There were several popular categories of *romanze*, and this one is called a *barcarola*. The word comes from *barca* (small boat),

and the songs are reminiscent of those that Venetian gondoliers sing. A *barcarola* is usually in a swaying 6/8 meter, and the words are often invitations to an evening boat ride.

Five other songs by Colbran are found in *Una voce poco fa* by Patricia Adkins Chiti, an anthology of songs composed by nine women, all of whom not only sang in premieres of Rossini operas but were also active, published composers (Rome: Garamond, 1992).

Colbran gave no dynamic markings except the crescendo in m8, leaving all other decisions to the performers. The harmonies in measures 21-22 are unusually rich for this period.

Sources

(1) *Passatempi musicali* (Naples: B. Girard [October 1824]), pages 12–13, Biblioteca del Conservatorio di San Pietro a Majella, Naples. Maestro Alessandro Manuali of Rome kindly obtained a photocopy of the first edition for this research. Voice part in treble clef. Key: G Major. (The Naples conservatory library believes this to be the first printing.)

(2) No. 39 (of 46 songs for voice and piano by various composers) in *Il Trovatore italiano, No. 38* (Milano: E. & P. Artaria, 1833), Canto e Piano 40–1, Milan.

(3) *Passatempi musicali,* edited by Ignazio Macchiarella (Bologna: Ut Orpheus Edizioni, 1998). Prof. Macchiarella supplies the information that *Passatempi musicali* was the title of a series of small collections that was published between 1824 and 1865 by Girard and by his successors, the Cottraus. He believed his source to be the first printing, but there are a number of discrepancies from sources (1) and (2).

Già la notte s'avvicina (Barcarola)

Pietro Metastasio

Isabella Colbran-Rossini
Edited by John Glenn Paton
(Range: D4–G5)

(a) Suggested tempo: ♩. = 60–64

(b) The Ricordi edition has G4 here, but D5 provides a better continuation.

(c) The Girard edition has a G3 on the fourth eighth note, probably a misprint.

(d) The repeat indications are present in the sources, but should be considered optional.

Translation: Night is coming O, Come, my beloved Nice, and breathe the cool breezes of the quiet seaside.
One cannot imagine

how delightful it is if he has not rested on this sand, now that a slight breeze is gently rippling the sea.

Non giova il sospirar

/non dʒɔːva sospiɾaɾ/

Sighing is of No Use

Nicola Vaccai (1790–1848)
/nikɔːla vakːkai/

non dʒɔːva_il   sospiɾaɾ, nɔ
1. **Non giova   il   sospirar, no,**
Not is-useful the sighing,   no,

non   lagrimaɾ per me
2. **Non lagrimar per me.**
don't weep   for me.

tiɾsi   pju   tuːo nonɛ
3. **Tirsi   più   tuo non è,**
Thyrsis anymore yours not is,

likɔːɾinfiːda
4. **Licori infida;**
Licori unfaithful;

gɔːdi   del nwɔːvo_amoɾ
5. **Godi   del nuovo   amor.**
you-are-enjoying a new   love.

trovera tiɾsi_aŋkoɾ
6. **Troverà Tirsi ancor**
Will-find Tirsi yet

ninfa   se non pju bɛlːla
7. **Ninfa, se non più bella,**
nymph, if not more beautiful,

almen di te pju fiːda   si
8. **Almen di te più fida,   sì.**
at-least than you more faithful, yes.

Poetic Background

"Don't cry for me. You have a new love and I can find one, too, perhaps not better looking, but at least more faithful than you."

For information about the poet please read the commentary on the song by Righini.

This text comes from one of Metastasio's lighter works, *L'Angelica*, a *serenata*, which probably means an evening entertainment shorter and less elaborate than a full opera. Metastasio apparently wrote this in Naples, and its first musical setting was by Nicola Pórpora in 1720.

The singer is Tirsi, addressing his frivolous girl friend, Licori. Their names come from the same tradition of ancient Greek pastoral poetry that was mentioned on page 00 in relation to the song *"Amarilli, mia bella."* In pastoral poetry, rural people are supposed to have simpler and more sincere feelings than city dwellers, but they have time for flirtation. Both Italian and English pastoral poetry used such names as Amarylis and Chloe either for fictional characters or as stand-ins for real people whom the poet did not wish to name. Licori's name occurs in other poems as Clori.

Line 1: The playful repetitions of *nò, nò* and *sí, sí* are Vaccai's additions, not Metastasio's text.

Musical Background

This song shows the sense of humor of a musician who is best remembered as a pedagogue. As the head of the conservatory at Milan, Vaccai introduced the idea of student performances of operas (as had already been done in Naples) and broadened the repertoire performed by students. When he conducted Handel's *Messiah* at the conservatory, there was a furor that caused him to resign.

This song was composed after Vaccai retired to his home at Pesaro, where he continued to teach and compose industriously. It is called a *canzonetta veneziana*, little Venetian song, perhaps because Venice is associated with fun, masquerades and, therefore, switching lovers.

The music is written in short, 3/8 measures; it will be lighter and more graceful if the singer thinks in four-measure phrases with the 1st and 3rd as upbeats to the stronger 2nd and 4th measures. Observe the articulation markings, including an expressive slur in m5, a staccato in m6, beat 3, and the strong emphases in m13.

The dynamic markings are all original with Vaccai.

Source

"Non giova il sospirar," canzonetta veneziana (Paris: Pacini, ca. 1846), Milan. For voice (treble clef) and piano. Key: Bb Major

Non giova il sospirar *(Canzonetta veneziana)*

Pietro Metastasio

Nicola Vaccai
Edited by John Glenn Paton
(Range: E4–F4)

ⓐ Suggested tempo: ♪ = 136–148. *Andantino*, as Vaccai uses it, is between *andante* and *moderato*.

Translation: Sighing does no good; don't weep for me. I am no longer yours.

You have a new lover. I will find one, too— if not more beautiful, then at least more faithful than you are.

Chi m'ascolta il canto usato?

/ki maskɔlta il kanto uzaːto/

Whoever Me-hears the Singing Customary

Gioachino Rossini (1792–1868)

/dʒoakiːno rosːsiːni/

ki	mascolta il	kanto	uzaːto
1. **Chi**	**m'ascolta il**	**canto**	**usato**
Whoever	me-hears the	singing	customary

ljeːto	ʃɔʎːʎere	talor
2. **Lieto**	**sciogliere**	**talor**
happy	release	sometimes

kredeɾa	kio	siːa beaːto
3. **Crederà**	**ch'io**	**sia beato,**
will-believe	that-I	am blessed,

ke a	mjɛi voːti	arːriːdaːmor
4. **Che a**	**miei voti**	**arrida amor.**
that on my	vows	smiles love.

noːnɛ	ver	tʃerko kol	kanto
5. **Non è**	**ver!**	**Cerco col**	**canto**
Not it-is	true!	I-seek with the	song

di sfogaɾ	il mio martir
6. **Di sfogar**	**il mio martir.**
to give-vent-to—	my suffering.

vɔ	tʃelando ad	altril	pjanto
7. **Vo**	**celando ad**	**altri il**	**pianto,**
I-am	hiding	from others	the tears,

interːrompo il	mio martir
8. **Interrompo il**	**mio martir.**
I-suspend	— my suffering.

kanto amor	perke	kolɛːi
9. **Canto amor**	**perché**	**colei**
I-sing love	because	she

ke	kozi	mi fa	penar
10. **Che**	**così**	**mi fa**	**penar**
who	thus	me makes	suffer

del	mio dwɔl	de	maːli mjɛi
11. **Del**	**mio duol,**	**de'**	**mali miei**
about	my sorrow,	about	ills my,

mai	non sabːbja	ralːlegrar
12. **Mai**	**non s'abbia a**	**rallegrar.**
ever	not would-have to	rejoice.

e	kozi ʃemando il	fɔːko
13. **E**	**così scemando il**	**foco**
And	thus lessening	the fire

ke	rakːkjuːdo nel	mio	sen
14. **Che**	**racchiudo nel**	**mio**	**sen,**
that	I-enclose in	my	bosom,

vɔ	vedeɾ se a	pɔːko a	pɔːko
15. **Vo**	**veder se a**	**poco a**	**poco**
I-want	to-see if	by little	by little

kon	me baɾbaɾo	siaːmor
16. **Con**	**me barbaro**	**sia amor.**
toward	me cruel	will-be love.

Poetic Background

"My happy singing conceals my pain so that my lover won't know that she caused it. Perhaps the next time I fall in love won't be so bad."

Lines 1-2: *Chi m' ascolta...sciogliere*, whoever hears me release. Although *usato* modifies *canto*, customary singing, *lieto* describes the person singing; English would use an adverb, "happily," instead of an adjective.

Line 7: *Vo* before a gerund stands for *vado*, I go, hence: "I go around hiding…"

Line 15: *Vo* before an infinitive stands for *voglio*, I want.

Line 16: *Sia a-* will be sung in m103 and m107 with [i] as an eighth and [a] as a quarter because it signifies two syllables.

Musical Background

In 1818, when Rossini wrote this song, he was the musical director of the famous Teatro San Carlo in Naples. He had already composed the masterful comic operas that are still in today's operatic repertoire, including *Il barbiere di Siviglia* and *La Cenerentola*. It was about this time that he became the lover of the beautiful Isabella Colbran, the composer of *"Già la notte s'avvicina"* (No. 11 in this book). He married her in 1822.

Almost every Rossini song shows one or more unusual, even bizarre features. In this song a chromatically rising, syncopated melody, decorated with a quick trill in the third measure of the phrase, perfectly portrays the false exuberance of the unhappy lover. At the end of the middle section, where we might expect a vocal cadenza, the tables are turned: the singer holds a tone for eight measures, and it is the pianist who has brilliant arpeggios.

Source

Arietta per camera. (Napoli: Giuseppe Girard [1818]), Noseda V16/3, Milan. For voice (soprano clef) and piano. Key: D Major.

Chi m'ascolta il canto usato

Poet unknown

Gioachino Rossini
Edited by John Glenn Paton
(Range: D4–F♯5)

ⓐ Suggested tempo: ♪ = 144–160.

ⓑ Trills in this song begin on the printed note (not the upper neighbor). They will be very short, probably just one alternation with the upper neighbor (like an inverted mordent) because of the quick tempo.

Translation: Whoever hears my customary song ringing out happily

cre - de - rà ch'io si - a be - a - to, che a mi εi vo - ti

ar - ri - da a - mor.

Non è ver! Cer - co col can - to di sfo - gar il mio mar -

sometimes would think that I'm ecstatic, that love is smiling on my wooing.
It's not true! I am trying to hide my pain by singing.

I go around hiding my tears from others; I'm taking a break from sadness.
I sing in praise of love so that the lover who hurt me

miɛ - i mai non s'ab - bia a ral - le - grar,

a — ral - le - grar,

a — ral - le - grar.

E co - sì sce -

will not have cause to rejoice about my pain and my ills. And so,

man-do il fo - co che rac - chiu - do nel___ mi - o sen, vɔ ve -

der se a pɔ-co a pɔ-co con me bar-ba - ro___ si'_ a - mor,

ⓒ
sia a - mor,

sia a - mor.

ⓒ Rossini indicated a *portamento*, which occurs when a slur connects two notes on different pitches that have two syllables of text. At the end of the first note the voice moves quickly to the pitch of the second note before changing to the second syllable. It was Vaccai's opinion that the voice should not slide between the two pitches but make the pitch change cleanly. Later in the 1800s a sliding *portamento* certainly became the standard.

On the long notes in m103 and m107 it may be effective to articulate the two /a/ vowels, although Rossini did not give them separate notes.

as the fire in my bosom is cooling down, I want to see little by little whether love will always be so cruel to me.

La Dichiarazione

[ka dikjaratːtsjoːne]

The Declaration

Gioachino Rossini (1792–1868)

kiːo mai vi pɔsːsa laʃːʃar damaːre
1. **Ch'io mai vi possa lasciar d'amare,**
That-I ever you could stop   loving,

nɔ nol   kredeːte pupilːle kaːre
2. **No, nol   credete, pupille care;**
no, not-it believe, eyes   dear.

ne men per dʒɔːko vinganːnerɔ
3. **Ne men per gioco v'ingannerò.**
Not even for joke   you-I-will-deceive.

voi foste   sjɛːte le miːe favilːle
4. **Voi foste e siete le mie faville,**
You were and are   — my   sparks,

e   voi sareːte kaːre pupilːle
5. **E   voi sarete, care pupille,**
and you will-be, dear   pupils,

il mio bɛl   fɔːko finkio   vivrɔ
6. **Il mio bel   foco finch'io   vivrò.**
— my beautiful fire   as-long-as-I shall-live.

Poetic Background

"I could never stop loving you, and I would never deceive you, even in fun."

For information about the poet please see the commentary to the song by Righini.

This poem comes from *Siroe, re di Persia,* an opera libretto that Metastasio wrote for the composer Leonardo Vinci (it was subsequently set by 33 other composers, including Vivaldi and Handel). The premiere was in Venice in 1726 with Metastasio's favorite soprano, Marianna Bulgarelli Benti, in a leading role. The plot of the opera concerns events in Persia in 628 C.E.

Emira, a foreign princess who has spent most of the opera disguised as a man, sings this to Prince Siroe at a time when both are in prison. Ultimately, Siroe and Emira achieve justice and become the king and queen of Persia.

Line 1: *vi,* is a plural pronoun, addressed to the beloved's eyes.

Line 2: *nol* is a poetic form, a contraction of *non il* or *non lo.* The L must be heard clearly.

Pupille is a figure of speech called synecdoche, in which a part (pupils) stands for the whole (eyes).

Line 3: *ne men* is one word in modern Italian, *nemmeno.* The [m] may be sung as [mːm] if the singer finds it comfortable.

Line 4: *mie,* for clarity, may be sung as two syllables in m57, with *–e* on the 16th note.

Faville is a metaphor, a figure of speech in which one thing stands for another; sparks stand for the beloved's sparkling glances.

Line 6: *mio* is not divided between the two 8ths in m68 because the tempo allows time to slur the [i] and add the [o] at the end of the diphthong.

Foco is a metaphor for love. The modern Italian word is *fuoco.*

Finché means both "until" and "as long as."

Musical Background

When Rossini wrote this song in 1834, he had separated from his wife and was living in Paris. He had declared a willingness to write for the Opéra, but had not done so since his *Guillaume Tell* (William Tell) five years earlier. Rossini had received a lifetime pension from the king of France, but the king had been deposed. Rossini was engaged in a stressful legal battle to continue the pension, which was ultimately restored. During this time he was often ill and was nursed by Olympe Pélissier, whom he married after Isabella died.

In the poem the lover promises never to be deceitful, even as a joke, but Rossini repeats *gioco* so emphatically that he is obviously thinking of other kinds of playfulness. He wrote another setting of the same poem, called *"La Promessa,"* in a group of songs called *Soirées musicales* (Musical Evenings, 1835). Both songs are lively and graceful and filled with musical humor.

Like many other songs in 3/8 time, this one will be lighter and more pleasing if the first measure of the melody (m20) is treated as an upbeat to the next measure, the third as an upbeat to the fourth, and so on. If all of the measures are stressed equally, the result will be too heavy as a result of the frequent downbeats.

Source

Quatre ariettes italiennes (Paris: Bonoldi, ca. 1847), A/30/51/4/6, Milan. For voice (treble clef) and piano. Key: E♭ Major. (There was reportedly an earlier edition of this song, Milan: Ricordi, ca. 1835.)

La Dichiarazione

Pietro Metastasio

Gioachino Rossini
Edited by John Glenn Paton
(Range: E♭4–A♭5)

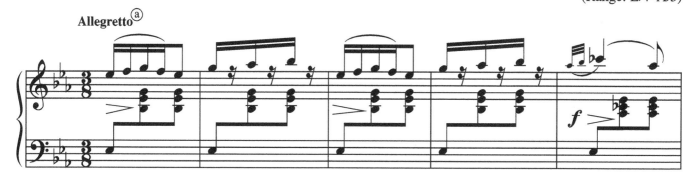

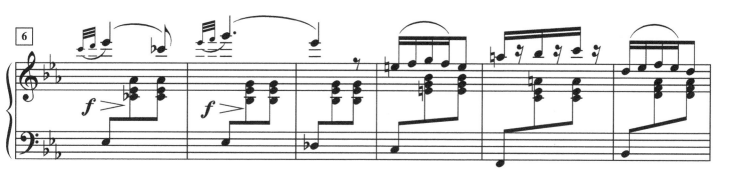

Ch'io mai vi pos - sa la - sciar d'a - ma - re,

ⓐ Suggested tempo: ♩ = 146–160.

Translation: That I could ever stop loving you,

no, nol cre - de - te, pu - pil - le ca - re; ne

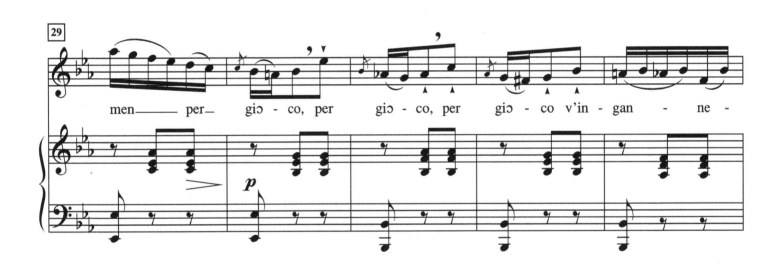

men _____ per _____ gio - co, per gio - co, per gio - co v'in - gan - ne -

rò, no, no, ne men _____

dear eyes— do not believe it; I would not deceive you, even in play.

You are and have always been sparkling for me, dear eyes, and you will be my love for as long as I live.

80 fin - ch'io vi vrò, fin - ch'io vi -

84 vrò, fin - ch'io vi - vrò.

90 Ch'io mai vi pos - sa la - sciar d'a - ma - re, no, nol cre - de - te,

96 pu - pil - le ca - re; ne men___ per___ gio - co, per gio - co, per___

La pastorella dell'alpi

/la pastorɛlːla delːlalpi/

The Shepherdess from the Mountains

Gioachino Rossini (1792–1868)

son bɛlːla   pastorɛlːla
1. **Son bella   pastorella**
   I-am beautiful shepherdess

ke ʃende onːɲi   matːtiːno
2. **Che scende   ogni   mattino**
   that descends every morning

edɔfːfre un tʃestelːliːno
3. **Ed offre un cestellino**
   and offers a   little-basket

di freske frutːta e   fjor
4. **Di fresche frutta e   fior.**
   of fresh   fruits   and flowers.

ki   vjɛːne al   priːmo alboːre
5. **Chi   viene   al   primo albore**
   Whoever comes at-the first   light-of-dawn

avra   vettsoːze roːze
6. **Avrà   vezzose   rose**
   will-have lovely   roses

e   poːma rudʒadoːze
7. **E   poma rugiadose—**
   and apples rosy—

veniːte al mio dʒardin au
8. **Venite al mio giardin. Ahu.**
   come   to my   garden.

ki   nel   notːturnorːroːre
9. **Chi   nel   notturno orrore**
   Whoever in-the nocturnal horror

zmarːri la bwɔːna via
10. **Smarrì la buona   via,**
    lost   the good   way

alːla kapanːna mia
11. **Alla   capanna   mia**
    at-the cabin   mine

ritroveɾa il   kamin
12. **Ritroverà   il   camin.**
    again-will-find the path.

veniːte o pasːsadːʒɛːɾo
13. **Venite, o passaggiero,**
    Come,   O traveler,

la pastorɛlːla ɛ kwa
14. **La pastorella   è qua,**
    the shepherdess is here,

ma il fjor   del suo pensjɛːɾo
15. **Ma il fior   del suo pensiero**
    but the flower of her thought

aduːno sol daɾa
16. **Ad uno sol   darà.**
    to one only she-will-give.

Poetic Background

"I come from the mountains to sell flowers. I help anyone, but I love only one."

Count Carlo Pepoli (1796–1881) lived much of his life in exile because he actively resisted the Austrian domination of northern Italy. He was a friend of the great poet Giacomo Leopardi. In Paris he wrote librettos for Bellini's *I Puritani* (The Puritans, 1835) and Vaccai's *Giovanna Gray* (Jane Gray, 1836). He also wrote eight of the poems in Rossini's *Soirées musicales*. He married Rossini's only pupil, the famous mezzo-soprano Marietta Alboni. After the unification of Italy he returned home to Bologna and served, like Verdi, in the parliament.

Title: *alpi* (mountain pastures) are not necessarily the Swiss Alps; the poet was probably thinking of the Italian Tyrol.

Line 2: *scende*, comes down from the mountains.

Line 4: *frutta* is an irregular plural, identical to the singular; *fior* is truncated from *fiori*.

Line 7: *poma rugiadose* is a rare and obsolete form, a feminine plural to the masculine *pomo rugiadoso*. (Modern Italian for "apple" is *mela*.)

Line 8: *ahu* is a discreet imitation of yodeling. The two vowels do not form a diphthong, and the H is silent.

Line 12: *camin* is an alternative form of *cammino* and permits a longer vowel on the high tone.

Musical Background

In French, *le soir* means evening, and *la soirée* is an elegant evening party. Rossini's name is often associated with such parties, and he hosted famous *soirées* at a later time in his life. In the 1830s, however, high society did not accept artists as social equals. Rossini would arrive with the singers whom he had contracted, enter by a side door, and perform. After compliments from the host, the artists would leave and receive their fees the next day (according to April Fitzlyon's *Maria Malibran*, London: Souvenir Press, 1987).

There are no specific dates for the eight songs and four duets that Rossini composed for his friends and that were published together as *Les soirées musicales*. They show clearly that Rossini's musical inspiration was still strong, even though this was a stressful time in his life (as described in the commentary to No. 16 in this volume).

Tirolese or, in French, *tyrolienne*, was a type of waltz-song, very popular in the 1800s for its association with the Tyrol, or western Alps. The Tyrolean Alps are now divided between Austria and Italy.

There are few differences between two sources, but source (2) changes Rossini's delicate ending with a forte marking for the last five chords of the piano interlude and postlude.

Sources

(1) No. 6 in *Les soirées musicales* (Mainz: B. Schott's Söhne, and simultaneously, Paris: Dépôt centrale de la musique, 1835.), M 46.470., Budapest. With a French translation released in Paris and a German translation released in Mainz. Dedication to Louise de Rotschild. Key: C Major.

(2) No. 6 in *Soirée musicale* (sic, Milano: Ricordi, 1878, still in print as *Serate musicali*). Subtitle: *"8 ariette e 4 duetti per lo studio del canto italiano."* With a French translation. Key: C Major.

La pastorella dell'alpi

Carlo Pepoli

Gioachino Rossini
Edited by John Glenn Paton
(Range: E4–G5)

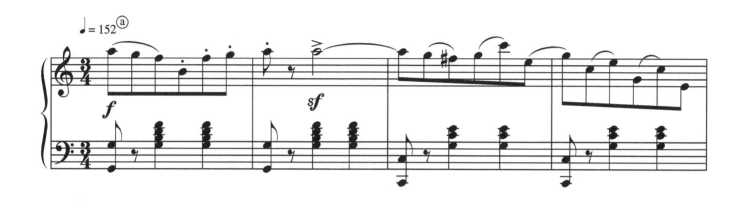

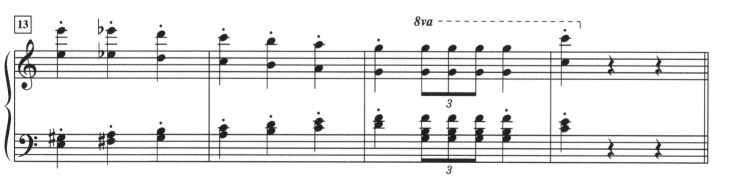

ⓐ The metronome marking comes from the composer, but should be interpreted with great freedom.

Translation: (1) I am the pretty shepherdess who comes down every morning and offers a basket of fresh fruits and flowers for sale. Whoever comes to me at dawn will have lovely roses

(2) Anyone who lost his way in the fearsome night can find the road again at my cottage. Come along, traveler, the shepherdess is here—

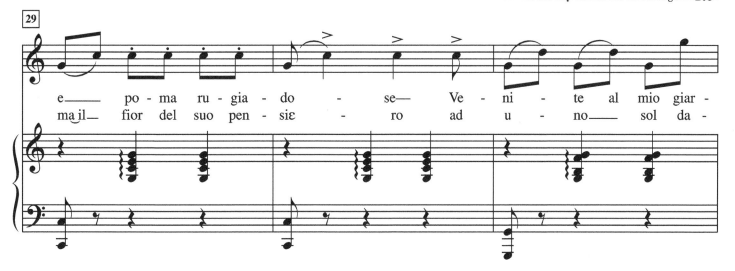

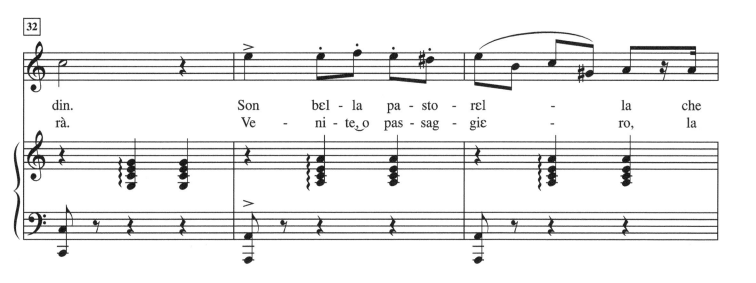

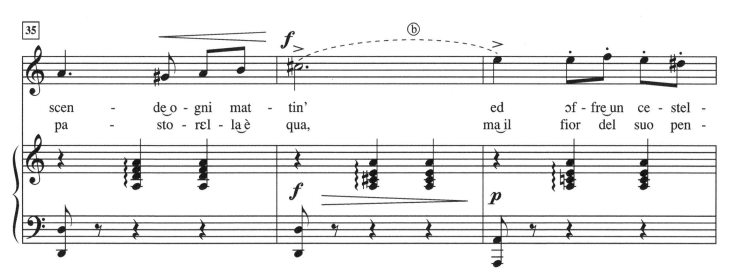

ⓑ Rossini indicated the *portamento*, which occurs when a slur connects two notes on different pitches that have two syllables of text. At the end of the first note the voice moves quickly to the pitch of the second note before changing to the second syllable. It was Vaccai's opinion (1834) that the voice should not slide between the two pitches, but make the pitch change cleanly. Later in the 1800s a sliding *portamento* certainly became the standard.

In the highly effective portamento here, the voice carries the syllable "–tin" up a minor third just before the first beat of m38 and continues without taking a breath. Also, in m44 the voice drops a minor tenth just before the first beat of m45.

and red apples. Come to my garden.
but she will give her very best thought to only one man!

© *Portato*, the combination of a slur with dots, originated in violin music, where it means the articulation of several notes on one bow stroke, either up or down. Since the bow does not stop moving, the notes are lightly connected but are distinguished by variation in the pressure of the bow. A similar effect is desired here: the tones are lightly connected but are made distinct by breath pressure.

Leonora
/leonɔːɾa/

Gaetano Donizetti (1797–1848)

partiːr	konvjɛːne	leonɔːɾadːdio	
1 Partir	**conviene:**	**Leonora, addio.**	
To-depart	is-necessary:	Leonora, farewell.	

dolʧeiːdol	mio	pjanʤer	perke
2 Dolce idol	**mio,**	**pianger**	**perché?**
Sweet idol	mine,	weep	why?

dolor	dun ʤorno	doloːr	mendaːʧe
3 Dolor	**d'un giorno,**	**dolor**	**mendace!**
Sorrow	of-a day,	sorrow	false!

nulːla	ɛ ffugaʧe	pju	ddelːlamoːr
4 Nulla	**è fugace**	**più**	**dell'amor.**
Nothing	is fleeting	more	than-love.

faɾa	ritorno la	veːlamaːta	
5 Farà	**ritorno la**	**vela amata;**	
Will	return the	sail loved;	

sol	te	kanʤaːta	ritroveɾa
6 Sol	**te**	**cangiata**	**ritroverà.**
only	you	changed	it-will-find.

alːlondeinfiːde	io	mabːbandoːno
7 All'onde infide	**io**	**m'abbandono.**
To-waves treacherous	I	myself-submit.

delːloːɾail	swɔːno	sul	kɔr	pjombɔ
8 Dell'ora	**il suono**	**sul**	**cor**	**piombò.**
Of-the-hour	the sound	on-the	heart	fell.

dɛ	gwaɾda il	ʧɛːlo vaːga	donʣɛlːla
9 Deh!	**guarda il**	**cielo, vaga**	**donzella;**
Please	look-at the	sky, lovely	young-woman

la	fiːda	stɛlːla maːi	non	kanʤɔ
10 La	**fida**	**stella mai**	**non**	**cangiò.**
The	faithful	star ever	not	changed.

per	nɔi rinːnɔːva la	kapineːɾa	
11 Per	**noi rinnova la**	**capinera**	
For	us renews the	blackcap	

di	primavɛːɾa la sua	kantsoːn	
12 Di	**primavera la sua**	**canzon.**	
of	spring — its	song.	

il	tɛmpo kruːdo tutːto distrudːʤe		
13 Il	**tempo crudo tutto distrugge,**		
The	time cruel all destroys,		

ma	ttutːto	fudːʤe per	ritornaːr
14 Ma	**tutto**	**fugge per**	**ritornar.**
but	everything	flees so-as-to	return.

Poetic Background

"I shall be out on the sea for a long time, but do not worry, Leonora. When I return we will love each other just as we do now."

Donizetti's style indication is *allegretto scherzoso,* moderately lively and playfully. This is a significant key to interpretation. This farewell is not tragic. When the sailor returns to Leonora, they will love each other again, even if nature and time have changed them somewhat.

Line 6: *sol te cangiata* has an implied meaning that is not expressly stated. The poet is thinking of faithfulness in love and answering an implied question from Leonora as to whether he will still love her when he returns from his voyage. He says that if she changes her mind while he is away, it will be only *(sol)* she who changes; his love will not change.

Line 11: *la capinera,* the blackcap, is a small European warbler, the male of which has a black head.

Musical Background

The music of *"Leonora"* was apparently published first with the title *"Canzonetta"* and the text *"Addio, Brunetta,*

son già lontano" (Farewell, Brunetta, I am already far away) in the Neapolitan journal *Il Sìbilo* (The Hiss), October 5, 1843. It was reproduced in *Donizetti Society Journal,* 1974, along with an amusing article by Jeremy Commons about how he rediscovered this obscure periodical.

According to UTET, *"Leonora"* was first published posthumously in *Dernières glanes musicales* (Last Musical Gleanings, Naples: B. Girard, no date). Standard reference works list both *"Addio, Brunetta"* and *"Leonora"* without noting that they are musically almost identical. The minor differences between them are detailed in *Donizetti: 20 Songs,* published by Alfred Publishing Co. Of the two settings, *"Leonora"* is published here because it is musically more complete and has a text that is wittier and more open to a variety of interpretations.

Source

"Leonora" (Milan: Ricordi, 1844), Milan. Original key: D Major.

Leonora

Poet unknown

Gaetano Donizetti
Edited by John Glenn Paton

Allegretto scherzoso

Par - tir con - vie - ne: Leo - no - ra, ad - di - o.
Al - l'on-de in - fi - de   io m'ab - ban - do - no.

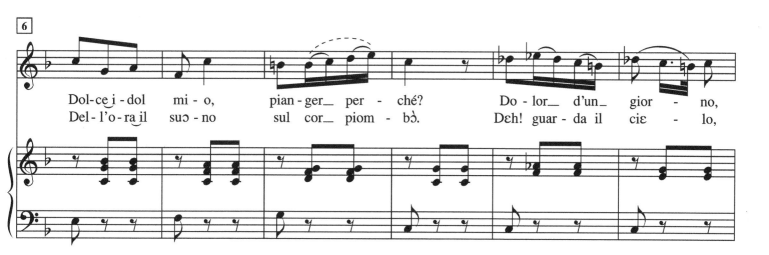

Dol-ce i-dol mi - o,   pian-ger_ per - ché?   Do - lor_ d'un_ gior - no,
Del - l'o - ra il suo - no   sul cor_ piom - bò.   Deh! guar - da il cie - lo,

do - lor_ men - da - ce!   Nul-la è fu - ga - ce più del - l'a - mor.
va - ga_ don - zɛl - la;   la fi - da_ stel - la mai non_ can - giò.

(a) Suggested tempo: ♩. = 74 – 82.

Literal translation: 1)   I must go; farewell, Leonora! Sweet idol of mine, why weep? One day's sorrow is a false sorrow! Nothing is more fleeting than love.

2)   I am entrusting myself to the treacherous sea; the hour of parting has sounded. Just look to the sky, lovely maiden; the faithful stars never change.

Refrain: The sail you love to see will return; you will have changed (but not I!). Leonora, farewell!

3) For us the warbler will renew its springtime singing. Time destroys all, but only so that all return anew.

ma - ta; sol te can - gia - ta ri - tro - ve - rà,

sol te___ can - gia - ta ri - tro - ve - rà. Ad - dio, Leo -

no - - - ra, Leo - nɔ - ra, ad - di -

- - - - - o, ad - di - o!

Se a te d'intorno scherza

/se a te dintorno skertsa/

If a Breeze Around You Plays

se a te dintorno skertsa
1 Se a te d'intorno scherza
If to you around plays

un nwɔːvo dʤefːfiret̠ːto
2 Un nuovo zeffiretto,
a new little-breeze,

non rɛsti o dio neglɛt̠ːto
3 Non resti, oh Dio, negletto!
not may-it-remain, oh God, neglected!

lakːkɔʎːʎi ɛun mio sospir
4 L'accogli: è un mio sospir.
Accept-it; it-is a my sigh.

kwel dʤefːfiro respiːra
5 Quel zeffiro respira
That breeze breathes

fiŋ ke ti dʤungal kɔːre
6 Fin che ti giunga al core;
Until that you it-reaches at-the heart;

ɛ un mesːsadːʤer damoːre
7 È un messagger d'amore,
it-is a messenger of-love,

di dʤɔːja e di martir
8 Di gioia, e di martir.
of joy, and of martyrdom.

Gaetano Donizetti (1797–1848)

Poetic Background

"Please accept the message of longing and love that I am sending to you."

Donizetti often chose texts that lend themselves to role-playing: the gondolier, the lad from the mountains, the gypsy girl. In contrast, this poem carries a message for anyone at all who is in love.

Musical Background

Beginning with an inverted altered chord, the rhythmically light introduction suits the poetic image of a gentle breeze. The vocal melody maintains a high tessitura throughout.

A Baroque composer would have used this eight-line text for a *da capo aria*, but Donizetti spins the legato melody in a unique and unpredictable way. Lines 1-4 of the poem form the first section, ending with a cadence on the dominant of the relative minor (m13). Lines 5-6 form a modulatory contrasting section. Lines 7-8 bring a return of the first melody, but it is ornamented and then extended, and the words are repeated with a variety of emotional inflections.

This song is included in *Donizetti: 20 Songs*, published by Alfred Publishing Co.

Sources

(1) Autograph manuscript, The Pierpont Morgan Library, New York City. Original key: F major. Voice part in soprano clef. Key: F. The single leaf of paper is printed with musical staves on both sides. The song is headed *"Romanza"* and signed "Donizetti."

(2) *"Se a te d'intorno scherza,"* published in the Neapolitan journal *Il Sìbilo* (The Hiss), April 4, 1844. It was reproduced in *Donizetti Society Journal,* 1974, along with an amusing article by Jeremy Commons about how he rediscovered this obscure periodical. He comments that its pages were small and that the print quality was not as clear as one would wish.

The single page of music is headed with the words *Romanza* and "from the album of Countess Angela Carradori." It was a common practice for musicians to respond to hospitality by copying a brief piece of music into the hostess's guest book. Just over the music are the words

"Property of the publisher Giuseppe Fabricatore." Donizetti spent the first six months of 1844 in Vienna, so it must have been Fabricatore who sold the song to *Il Sibilo*.

Since neither source was prepared for publication by Donizetti, the discrepancies between (1) and (2) cannot be finally resolved. The performer may choose between possibilities listed here.

Measure 4: (2) has a *diminuendo* rather than a *crescendo*.

Measure 11: (2) lacks the *accelerando*.

Measure 12, voice part: (1) has an ornament that is clearly written but is probably an error, nevertheless. The double-grace notes are the pitches F and E (in the original key of F), producing a lower neighbor figure that would be abnormal in the period. The alternative pitches D and E given in (2) are much more normal, and just as expressive. Notice that the stressed vowel [i] must be sung on the grace notes and sustained on the dotted quarter; the secondary vowel [o] occurs quickly at the end of the dotted quarter.

Measure 12, piano part: The somewhat unexpected notes on the first two beats are, however, quite clearly readable in both sources. Source (2) has a block chord in the piano on beat 3, followed by rests over which is a wide fermata. Source (1) has the broken chord figure shown in this edition with a wide fermata sign, just as he wrote it; the curved line embraces at least three notes, and the dot is between beats 3 and 4. This sign, which was also used by Schubert, shows that several notes are slowed down to accommodate the held tone in the voice. Fortunately, recent advances in music engraving allow us to re-introduce this useful symbol.

Measure 17, beat 4, piano part: (2) has a quarter rest in both hands.

Measure 21: (2) lacks the dynamic marking, as do measures 22, 23, 26 and 27.

Measure 24, piano part: On beat 1 source (2) has D in the left hand; source (1) has a note that can be read as either C or D. C is clearly preferable on stylistic grounds. On beat 4 the unexpected chord is given here as in (2); source (1) is unreadable at this point because of erasures and corrections.

Measure 32, piano part: (2) lacks the seventh of the chord on beat 3.

Se a te d'intorno scherza

Poet unknown

Gaetano Donizetti
Edited by John Glenn Paton

Se a te d'in-tor-no— scher-za un nuo-vo zef-fi-ret-to, non— re-sti, oh Dio, ne-glet-to! L'ac-co-gli: è un mio so-

ⓐ Suggested tempo: ♩ = 78–86.

Literal translation: If you feel a new breeze playing around you, do not let it be ignored. Accept it: it is a

sigh from me. That breeze keeps wafting until it reaches your heart. It is a messenger of love, of joy and of my suffering.

Che vuoi di più?

[ke vwɔi di pju]

What More Do You Want?

Gaetano Donizetti (1797–1848)

ke	vwɔi	di pju	non	splɛnde
1. Che	**vuoi**	**di più?**	**Non**	**splende**
What	do-you-want	of more?	Does-not	shine

ne	twɔi bɛʎːʎɔkːkil		soːle
2. Ne'	**tuoi begl'occhi**	**il**	**sole?**
in	your beautiful eyes	the	sun?

un	sospir tuo	non	rɛnde
3. Un	**sospir tuo**	**non**	**rende**
A	sigh yours	does-not	render

zgombro	di nuːbil		tʃɛl
4. Sgombro	**di nubi**	**il**	**ciel?**
clear	of clouds	the	sky?

ke	vwɔi	di pju	damoːre
5. Che	**vuoi**	**di più?**	**D'amore**
What	do-you-want	of more?	Of-love

a	te una viːta	io	dʒuːro	
6. A te	**una vita**	**io**	**giuro,**	
to you	a life	I	swear;	

mutarmin	pɛtːto il	kɔːre
7. Mutarmi in	**petto il**	**core**
to-change-me in	bosom the	heart

pur	non potraː	lavɛl nɔ
8. Pur	**non potrà**	**l'avel, no.**
indeed	not will-be-able	the-grave, no.

adinfjorar	la tɛrːra
9. Ad infiorar	**la terra**
To cover-with-flowers	the earth

koːmun beaːto eliːzo	
10. Com'un beato	**eliso,**
like-a blessed	Elysium,

a far dun swɔl di gwɛrːra	
11. A far d'un suol	**di guerra**
to make of-a land	of war

di paːtʃe un paradiːso	
12. Di pace un	**paradiso,**
of peace a	paradise,

mi basta un tuo sorːriːzo	
13. Mi basta un tuo	**sorriso.**
for-me is-enough a your	smile.

nɔ non vɔʎːʎio di pju	
14. No, non vogl'io	**di più.**
No, not wish-I	of more.

Poetic Background

"What more do you want? Haven't I promised you my whole life? I want nothing more than one of your smiles that turn earth into paradise." The poor lover has been accused of not loving intensely enough.

Sung by two women, the poem expresses the feelings of a single lover. Sung by a tenor and soprano, the poem portrays two lovers who are initially at odds but reach a harmonious expression of mutual love.

In measures 14–16 Donizetti inserted words that do not fit into the meter or the rhyme of the poem: *"Che? Parla... Dì..."* ("What? Speak... Say..."). These create a surprising bit of dramatic realism as one singer urges the other to express herself frankly.

Line 3: *non* is missing from source (1) but is needed for both meter and meaning.

Line 7: *eliso* (or *elisio*) was a delightful garden assigned in Greek mythology to the souls of virtuous persons after death.

Line 14: *vogl'io,* a contraction of *voglio io,* contains two stressed vowels. In m32 Donizetti acknowledges both stresses by placing *vo-* on an upward leap with an accent mark and *io* on a stronger beat. In m32, m38 and similar passages, Donizetti wrote *io* as one syllable slurred on two or three notes, but in m61 and m65, where a leap is involved, he wrote *i-o*. In m36 and similar passages, *io* is sung on a single note, as a diphthong.

Musical Background

In 1842 Donizetti was in Vienna to conduct the premiere of *Linda di Chamounix*, which had a great success. On May 24, following the third performance of *Linda*, Donizetti wrote in a letter that he had just "completed a little musical album (to pay for the trip)." This duet is the last of the seven numbers, which include five songs and two duets, all on texts by Guaita.

In source (1) the two voices are designated as *"voce seconda"* and *"voce prima,"* obviously two sopranos, as Donizetti dedicated the duet to two sisters. The text is romantic but completely genderless, which is somewhat rare in Italian. In source (2) the voices are designated as tenor and soprano.

Sources

(1) No. 7, *Ispirazioni viennesi* (Vienna: Pietro Mechetti, 1842), RGY 1422 Z, Budapest. Dedication: *"alle Sorelle Signore Matilde e Luigia Branca."* Key: A-flat Major.

(2) No. 7, *Inspirations viennoises*, (Milano: Ricordi, c1842), A-55-57–11/A, Milan.

Che vuoi di più?

Carlo Guaita

Gaetano Donizetti
Edited by John Glenn Paton
(Range: E♭4–A♭5)

ⓐ Suggested tempo: ♩ = 76-84. (M2 is *a piacere*, freely. The tempo resumes with the upbeat to m3).

ⓑ Notice the *portamento* connecting beat 3 to beat 4. *Portamenti* are also prominent in measures 4, 7, 9, 14, etc. A *portamento* occurs when a slur connects two notes on different pitches that have two syllables of text. At the end of the first note the voice moves quickly to the pitch of the second note before changing to the second syllable. Vaccai was among the writers who said that the voice should change the pitch cleanly, without sliding. Later in the 1800s a sliding *portamento* certainly became the standard.

Translation: What more do you want? Doesn't the sun shine in your eyes? Does not one sigh of yours clear away the clouds

from the sky? What more do you want? I swear to give you a life of love; even the grave cannot change my heart.

© Suggested tempo: ♩. = 74–80.

ⓓ Prolong the *a* of *basta* and add the *u* as a diphthong after beat 4. If *un* arrives on the beat, it will be too emphatic, changing the meaning from "a smile" to "one smile."

To make earth bloom like a blessed Elysium, to turn this world of war into a paradise, all I need is a smile of yours. I ask no more!

ba - - - sta, ah___ sì, mi ba - - - sta. Nɔ, nɔ, non vɔ -

ba - sta un tuo sor - ri - so. Nɔ, non vɔ-gl'io di più, non vɔ -

gl'i - o di___ più, nɔ, nɔ, nɔ.___

gl'io di più, nɔ, nɔ, nɔ, nɔ.___

___ Ad in - fio - rar la tɛr - ra co - m'un be - a - tǫ e -

___ Ad in - fio - rar la tɛr - ra co - m'un be - a - tǫ e -

ⓔ *Calando* means become slower and softer. The tempo resumes in m43.

Per pietà, bell'idol mio
/per pjeta bɛlːliːdol miːo /
For Pity, Beautiful Idol Mine

Vincenzo Bellini (1801–1835)
/vintʃɛntso belːliːni/

per pjeta bɛlːliːdol   miːo
1. **Per pietà, bell'idol   mio,**
For pity,   beautiful-idol mine,

non mi   dir kiːo soːno ingraːto
2. **Non mi   dir ch'io sono   ingrato:**
not to-me say that-I am   ungrateful.

infeliːtʃe   zventuraːto
3. **Infelice   e   sventurato,**
Unhappy and unlucky,

abːbastantsa il tʃɛl   mi fa
4. **Abbastanza il ciel   mi fa.**
enough   the heaven me makes.

se fedeːle a te   soniːo
5. **Se fedele a te   son'io,**
If faithful to you am-I,

se mi   strugːgo a twɔi bɛi   luːmi
6. **Se mi   struggo a' tuoi bei   lumi,**
if myself I-melt   for your beautiful eyes (lights),

salːlo amoːr   lo sanːno i   nuːmi
7. **Sallo   amor, lo sanno i   numi,**
knows-it love, it know   the gods,

il mio kɔre il tuo   lo sa
8. **Il mio core, il tuo   lo sa.**
— my heart, — yours it knows.

Poetic Background
"Please do not call me ungrateful. My love for you is clear."

This text is sung by the title character in the opera *Artaserse*. The libretto was written in 1730 by Pietro Metastasio (please read more about him on page 000) for the composer Leonardo Vinci. Successful from the beginning, the opera by Metastasio and Vinci was widely performed and greatly praised. Independently from Vinci's music, *Artaserse* was set to music by 62 other composers in the next 90 years.

The crown prince of Persia, named Artaxerxes in English, has learned that his father, King Xerxes, has been stabbed to death. Just as he is departing to seek the murderer, his fiancée, Semira, enters. Not knowing why he is disturbed, she accuses him of not loving her. He sings this aria to reassure her before he goes to seek revenge.

Line 7: *Sallo amor* = "love knows." The object "it," not required in English, is needed in Italian. Normal word order in prose would be *"amore lo sa."*

Line 7: *i numi* are non-Christian gods. Xerxes was murdered in 465 B.C.E.

Line 8: *Il mio core, il tuo lo sa*: "My heart knows it, your heart knows it." As in Line 7, "it" refers to the lover's faithfulness.

Musical Background
When Bellini published this *arietta* in 1829, he lived in Milan and moved in the highest social circles. He was handsome and charming and lived for months at a time in the homes of wealthy patrons. He had written two operas that were highly successful (although they did not survive long in the repertoire). Based on their success, he received larger fees than other composers and was able to live without the additional income from teaching or conducting.

Source
"Arietta V." from *Sei ariette per camera*, first edition (Milan: G. Ricordi, 1829), A-55–14–B–12, Milan. Dedication "to the excellent dilettante, Signora Marianna Pollini." For voice (soprano clef) and piano. Key: C minor.

Per pietà, bell'idol mio

Pietro Metastasio

Vincenzo Bellini
Edited by John Glenn Paton
(Range: E♭4–A♭5)

Per pie - tà,_____ bel-l'i-dol mi - o, non mi
dir ch'io so - no in-gra - to, non mi dir ch'io so - no in-gra-to. In-fe-
li - ce e sven-tu - ra - to,_____ ab - ba - stan - za il ciel_ mi_

(a) Suggested tempo: ♩ = 140–166.

(b) Bellini gave only three dynamic markings: here, m43 and m59. The singer needs to plan the dynamics to be sure that the entire song is not monotonously loud.

Translation: Please, my beautiful one, do not tell me that I am ungrateful. Heaven has already made me miserable enough.

If I am faithful to you, if I am dying of love for you—Love knows, the gods know, my heart and yours know these things, also.

cor, il tu-o lo—sa, sì,—— lo sa.— Per pie-tà,——— bel-l'i-dol mi - o, non mi dir ch'io so - no in-gra - to, non mi dir ch'io so - no in-gra - to. In-fe-li - ce, sven-tu-ra-to,— ab-ba-stan-za il ciel mi fa. Se fe-de-le a te so-n'i - o, se mi strug-go a' tuoi bei

Maggiore

© The singer has utmost freedom here, as to expressive character, timing and dynamics. A cadenza is possible here, or a beautiful effect could be created on the long tone by swelling and diminishing, a *messa di voce*.

ⓓ The *pp* is probably a mistake. Certainly, the voice part is vigorous and, in the editor's opinion, measures 61–63 must be played energetically.

Vaga luna, che inargenti
/ˈvaːga ˈluːna ke inardˈʒɛnti/
Lovely Moon, Spreading Silver

Vincenzo Bellini (1801–1835)

ˈvaːga ˈluːna ke inardˈʒɛnti
1. **Vaga luna, che inargenti**
Lovely moon, that silvers

ˈkwɛste ˈriːve   ˈkwesti ˈfjoːri
2. **Queste rive e   questi fiori,**
these   banks and these   flowers

ed inˈspiɾi ˈaʎːʎelemɛnti
3. **Ed inspiri agli elementi**
and inspires into the elements

il liŋgwadˈʒːo delˈlamor
4. **Il linguaggio   dell'amor;**
the language   of-love,

testimˈɔnjor ˈsɛi tu ˈsoːla
5. **Testimonio or sei tu sola**
witness now   are you alone

del ˈmio ˈfɛrvido deˈziɾ
6. **Del mio fervido desir,**
of   my   fervent   desire,

ˈeda ˈlɛi ke minːnamoːra
7. **Ed a lei che m'innamora**
and to her that me-inflames-to-love

ˈkonta i ˈpalpiti ˈe i   sosˈpir
8. **Conta i   palpiti   e   i   sospir.**
tell   the trembling and the sighs.

ˈdilːle   pur ke lontanˈantsa
9. **Dille   pur che lontananza**
Say-to-her then that distance

il ˈmio dwɔl non pwɔ leˈnir
10. **Il mio duol   non può lenir,**
— my   sorrow not can   relieve,

ke se ˈnuːtro ˈuːna speˈrantsa
11. **Che se nutro   una speranza,**
that if I-harbor a   hope,

ˈelːla ɛ sol nelːlavːveˈnir
12. **Ella è sol   nell'avvenir.**
it   is only in-the-future.

ˈdilːle   pur ke ˈdʒorno e   ˈseːra
13. **Dille   pur che giorno e   sera**
Say-to-her then that day   and evening

ˈkonto ˈloːre   del doˈlor
14. **Conto l'ore   del dolor,**
I-count the hours of   sorrow,

ke ˈuːna ˈspɛːme luziŋgˈjɛɾa
15. **Che una speme   lusinghiera**
that a   hope   flattering

mi konˈfɔrta nelːlaˈmor
16. **Mi conforta   nell'amor.**
me comforts   in-love.

Poetic Background

"Dear moon, tell my beloved that I am sorrowing alone, hoping that she will come back to me."

The rhyme scheme of this poem is very regular, except that lines 2 and 4 do not rhyme. Possibly, they originally rhymed, and line 4 ended with *"degli amori."* Bellini may have changed the words to give the same rhythm to lines 4 and 12, which have the same melody.

Line 3: *elementi* is used figuratively to mean the natural environment.

Line 5: *tu* is the moon.

Line 8: *conta*, tell, is a poetic use of *contare*; a more common word would be *raccontare*.

Line 9: *dille* is a contraction of *dì a lei*.

Line 14: *conto*, I count, is the normal use of *contare*.

Musical Background

Early sources call this song a *romanzetta*. It shares the Romantic world of the Chopin nocturnes: the solitary lover pouring out his longing to the night sky. Artists of the 1830s put a high value on sentiment and sensitivity. The simplicity of this song's melody invites the singer and pianist to shape it into something flexible, imaginative and full of feeling.

Pauline Viardot, one of the great singer-composers of the 1800s, included *"Vaga luna"* in a collection that she edited called *Echos d'Italie*, vol. 1 (Durand, 186_?). Viardot's edition is long out of print but may be found in major libraries. It is worth studying to see the changes that she made in the melody when she sang it.

Source

Tre ariette inedite (Milan: Ricordi, May 1838), A55–14-B–15, Milan. Key: Ab Major. (The first two songs in the set were *"Il fervido desiderio"* and *"Dolente immagine di Fille mia."* In spite of being called "unpublished ariettas," all three songs had been published previously.)

Vaga luna, che inargenti

Poet unknown

Vincenzo Bellini
(Range: C4–E♭5)

ⓐ Suggested tempo: ♩ = 60-66

Translation: Lovely moon, that spreads silver on these shores and these flowers and

breathes the language of love into Nature, you alone are the witness of my fervent love; tell her whom I love about my

ⓑ On beat 2 Viardot's edition has A♭-B♭.

ⓒ In Viardot's edition the quarter note is an a-flat followed by a b-flat (m47 and m49 the same).

trembling and sighs. Say

pur che lon - ta - nan - za il mio duol non puo' le -

nir,＿＿＿＿ che se nu - tro, se nu-tro u-na spe-ran - za, el-la è

sol, sì, el-la è sol nel-l'av-ve - nir. Dil-le pur che gior-no e

se - ra con-to l'o - re del do - lor, che u-na

to her that distance does not lessen my pain and that if I cling to hope, it is only for the future. Say to her that both day
and night my hours pass in sorrow, that an

spɛ - me ̯u-na spɛ-me lu-sin-ghiɛ - ra   mi con - for - ta, mi con-for-ta nel-l'a -

mor, che ̯u - na spɛ - me lu - sin - ghiɛ-ra mi con-for-ta nel - l'a -

mor, che ̯u - na spɛ - me lu - sin - ghiɛ-ra mi con - for - ta nel - l'a -

mor, nel - l'a - mor, nel - l'a - mor.

enticing hope comforts me in my love.

Il Zeffiro

/il dzɛfːfiro/
The Zephyr

Vincenzo Bellini (1801–1835)

ventitʃɛl   ke laːli   dɔːro
1. **Venticel,   che l'ali   d'oro**
   Little-breeze, that the-wings of-gold

vai   batːtɛndo a me dapːprɛsːso
2. **Vai   battendo a me d'appresso,**
   you-are beating   to me all-around,

se vedɛstil   mio tezɔːro
3. **Se vedesti   il mio tesoro,**
   if you-should-see the my   treasure,

dimːmi o kaːro dimmi ovɛ
4. **Dimmi, o caro,   dimmi ov'è.**
   tell-me, o dear,   tell-me where-he-is.

a   se il   lɔkovei sodːdʒorna
5. **Ah! se il   loco   ov'ei   soggiorna**
   Ah, if the place   where-he is-staying

penetrar non mɛ   kontʃɛsːso
6. **Penetrar non m'è   concesso,**
   to-enter not to-me-is allowed,

dzefːfirɛtːto a lui ritorna
7. **Zeffiretto,   a lui ritorna**
   Little-breeze, to him return

e   favɛlːlaʎːʎi per me
8. **E   favellagli   per me.**
   and speak-to-him for me.

Poetic Background

"Find my love, little breeze, and wherever he is, please remind him of me."

A zephyr is a gentle breeze, usually from the west.

Title: *zeffiro* is preceded by *lo* in modern Italian, pronounced [lodːdzefːfiro].

Line 5: *ov'ei* is a contraction of two shortened words. *Ove* is a form of *dove*, and *ei* is a form of *egli*.

Line 8: *favellagli* combines an imperative verb with an indirect object *gli*.

Musical Background

This arietta is not included in standard reference books that list Bellini's works, but it appears in two early sources that appear to be reliable.

The source used for this edition is a version in D minor found in the library of the Conservatory in Milan. Somewhat roughly and hastily written, the score is regarded by the library as an autograph manuscript of Bellini's. The text is written in a finer handwriting. The title page, written by a third person, says *"Il Zeffiro / Arietta inedita / Musica del Maestro Bellini."* Probably the designation "unpublished arietta" would only have been added after Bellini's death.

Musicologist Riccardo Allorto has published a version in E minor in *Arie, Ariette e Romanze* (Milan: Ricordi, 1998). His source was a printed collection found in the Biblioteca Marciana in Venice. He says that the title page is missing and the book cannot be dated. In Allorto's version, the introduction is *forte* and there are other dynamic markings that may have been added by him.

Allorto mentions a discovery by musicologist Francesco Cesari that the melody of *"Il Zeffiro"* resembles an aria in Bellini's opera *La Straniera* (The Stranger, 1829). The aria, *"Sventurato il cor,"* is the entrance aria of the soprano, named Alaide. The aria and the song resemble each other only in the first nine notes and are completely different otherwise. It is not clear whether the song was composed before or after the opera.

Source

Manuscript A-55–14-B-31, Milan. Six pages, with music on pages 2-5. (Page 6 contains a sketch of a melody, but without a clef, key or meter signature.) For voice (soprano clef) and piano. Key: D minor.

Il Zeffiro

Poet unknown

Vincenzo Bellini
(Range: D#4–G5)

ⓐ Suggested tempo: ♪ = 126 - 140

Translation: Dear breeze, beating your golden wings around me, if

you should see my beloved, tell me, dear one, tell me where he is. If he is staying in some place that I cannot enter, dear breeze, speak to him on my behalf.

pres - so, se ve - de - sti il mio te - so - ro, dim - mi, o ca - ro, dim - mi o -

v'è.   Ah! se il lo - co o - v'ei sog - gior - na pe - ne - trar non m'è con -

ces - so, zef - fi - ret - to, a lui ri - tor - na e fa - vel - la - gli__ per

me, e fa - vel - la - gli__ per__ me.

L'Allegro
The Happy One

Marietta Brambilla (1807–1875)

poike ʎiʎanːni son ridɛnti
1. Poiché gli anni son ridenti,
Since the years are smiling,

poike amoːr tʃi skalda il seːno
2. Poiché amor ci scalda il seno,
since love for-us warms-up the bosom,

non perdjaːmo i bɛi momɛnti
3. Non perdiamo i bei momenti,
not let-us-lose the beautiful moments,

koʎːʎam loːre del pjatʃer
4. Cogliam l'ore del piacer.
let-us-gather the-hours of pleasure.

a ke dʒoːva kol pensjɛːro
5. A che giova col pensiero
For what serves with thought

ir vagando nel futuːro
6. Ir vagando nel futuro?
to-go wandering into-the future?

pɛnsil fɔlːle al di ventuːro
7. Pensi il folle al dì venturo,
Let-think the crazy-man of-the day coming,

del prezɛnte vɔ godeɾ
8. Del presente vo' goder.
of-the present I-want to-enjoy.

koːme raːpida rivjɛːɾa
9. Come rapida riviera
Like rapids of-a-river

pasːsa il flutːto delːla viːta
10. Passa il flutto della vita,
passes the flood of life,

e ki sa se kwɛsta seːɾa
11. E chi sa, se questa sera
and who knows if this evening

noi saɾeːmo aŋkoːɾ kwadːdʒu
12. Noi saremo ancor quaggiù!
we will-be still down-here.

Poetic Background
"This is the good time of life; I want to enjoy it fully because no one knows how long it will last."

Only the poet's first initial and family name are still known.

Line 4: *cogliamo* usually means to gather flowers.

Line 6: *ir = andare.* The verb *ire* comes from Latin and is not in common use.

Line 8: *vo'* is a contraction of *voglio.*

Line 9: *rapida* is not the adjective meaning quick, but a noun meaning the rapids; *riviera* is an adjective meaning pertaining to a river.

Line 11: *chi sa* may be pronounced with [sːs].

Line 12: *quaggiù* is a compound formed of *qua giù,* here below, meaning on earth and not in heaven. The double *gg* represents the textual doubling that is suggested for *chi sa.*

Musical Background
While every singer needs musical skills, few singers are such thoroughly trained and creative musicians that they also succeed as composers. Marietta Brambilla was one who had an international singing career and also excelled as a teacher and composer.

Three other songs and a duet by Brambilla are found in *Una voce poco fa...* by Patricia Adkins Chiti, an anthology of songs composed by nine women, all of whom not only sang in premieres of Rossini operas but were also active,

published composers (Rome: Garamond, 1992). As an evaluation of Brambilla's work, Adkins Chiti writes: "Although these works are not extraordinarily original..., the composer fully understood and practiced the Italian 'belcanto' method of singing, and these songs, certainly not easy from a technical point of view, require the interpretation of accomplished singers... Marietta Brambilla's songs, once performed by her sister and her niece, merit a place in the repertoire of every would-be Diva!" The sister mentioned was Teresa Brambilla, the first heroine of Verdi's *Rigoletto,* and the niece was Teresina Brambilla, who sang in the operas of her husband, Amilcare Ponchielli. Both were Marietta Brambilla's students.

Brambilla's song is the first one in this book to come from a collection of *melodie.* Within the collection, *"L'Allegro"* is called a *ballata,* a term that is applied to a light-hearted song in a dance-like rhythm.

The title page of Brambilla's *melodie* identifies her as *"Artista del Teatro Reale Italiano di Parigi,"* better known as *Théatre Royal Italien* in Paris.

Source
L'Allegro, Ballata per Baritono o Contralto, No. 2 of *Souvenir des Alpes, Raccolta di sei melodie italiane* (Milan: Giovanni Ricordi, February 1847), A55-26-2, Milan. Dedication to Augusta de Montleart. Original key: Db Major.

L'Allegro

M. Maggioni

Marietta Brambilla
(Range: Bb3–F5)

Poi-ché gli an - ni son— ri-

dɛn - ti, poi-ché a - mor ci scal - da il se - no, non per -

dia - mo i bɛi mo-men - ti, co - gliam l'o - re del___ pia -

ⓐ Suggested tempo: ♪= 148 –166. Notice that the composer made a distinction between horizontal accent marks used for notes that are legato and fully sustained and vertical accent marks for notes that are non-legato.

ⓑ "With brilliance."

ⓒ "Long" is used here instead of a fermata sign. The accompaniment is marked "with the voice" and the entire measure is prolonged. M14 is *a tempo.*

Translation: As long as our years are smiling and love warms our hearts, let's not waste the beautiful moments, let us treasure the hours of pleasure.

What good it is to let our thoughts wander into the future? Let fools think of the future; I want to enjoy the present.

ⓓ The word *io* is introduced here for emphasis. Sing the three notes as triplet 32nds with *i-* slurred on the first two notes.

Co-me ra - pi-da ri - viɛ-ra passa il
flut - to del - la vi - ta, e chi sa, se que - sta
se - ra noi sa - re - mo an - cor quag - giù! e chi sa, se que - sta
se-ra noi____ sa - re - mo an - cor quag - giù! e chi sa, se que - sta____

ⓔ Suggested tempo: ♩ = 90 – 98.

ⓕ "At pleasure," that is, slowly and freely. The *portamento* means that the voice drops an octave on the syllable *que-*
just before singing *sta*.

Life passes like the rapids of a river, and who knows if we will still be here this evening?

(g) Treat the grace note as an appoggiatura, that is, sing *se-* as an eighth note a half-step higher than written. (In the 1800s, a slash through the stem did not necessarily indicate an acciaccatura. That interpretation became common in the 1900s.)

(h) Again, the word *lunga* takes the place of a fermata sign. There are two possible ways to perform this measure. (1) Breathe after the first *quaggiù* and use the *portamento* to connect the second *quaggiù* to *poiché*; or (2) Sing *quaggiù, quaggiù* with the detached articulation that is indicated by the vertical accents, but take a breath *after* singing the portamento and before singing *poiché*. A breath after a portamento is seldom written in a score, but Italian tradition permits it. Notice that there is *no* portamento after the long tone in m63.

In solitaria stanza
[in solitaːrja stantsa]
In A Solitary Room

Giuseppe Verdi (1813–1901)
/dʒuzɛpːpe vɛrdi/

in solitaːrja stantsa
1. In solitaria   stanza
In solitary   room

laŋgwe   per dɔʎːʎatroːtʃe
2. Langue   per doglia atroce—
she-languishes from torment atrocious—

ilːlabbro ɛ sɛntsa voːtʃe
3. Il   labbro è senza   voce,
the lip   is without voice,

sɛntsa respiːro il   sen
4. Senza   respiro il sen,
without breath   the bosom,

koːme in dezɛrtajwɔːla
5. Come in deserta aiuola
As   in deserted flower-bed

ke   di rudʒaːde ɛ priːva
6. Che di rugiade è priva
which of dews   is deprived

sotːto alla vampa   estiːva
7. Sotto alla vampa   estiva
under   the burning-heat of-summer

mɔlːle nartʃiːzo zvjɛn
8. Molle narciso   svien.
weak   narcissus faints.

io dalːlafːfanːnopːprɛsːso
9. Io, dall'affanno   oppresso,
I, by breathlessness oppressed,

korːro per   vie   rimɔːte
10. Corro per   vie   rimote
run   through streets remote

e   griːdo in   swɔn ke pwɔːte
11. E   grido in   suon che puote
and I-shout with sound that can

le ruːpi   intenerir
12. Le rupi   intenerir:
the steep-rocky-cliffs turn-soft:

salvaːte o dɛi   pjetoːzi
13. Salvate, o Dei pietosi,
Save,   o gods merciful,

kwelːla beltà tʃelɛste
14. Quella beltà celeste!
that   beauty heavenly!

voi forse   non saprɛste
15. Voi forse   non sapreste
You perhaps not   would-know-how

unaltra irɛːne ordir
16. Un'altra Irene ordir!
another Irene to-create.

Poetic Background

"She is dying alone in her room. I run through the streets, crying out to the gods: 'Save my beloved from dying. She could never be replaced.'"

Jacopo Andrea Vittorelli (1749–1835) was a Venetian poet, but little is known about his life. His poetry is considered to be in a pastoral or "Arcadian" tradition. Franz Schubert set two of his poems to music in the course of his studies with Antonio Salieri.

Verdi chose melancholy poems for all his first songs, suiting a morbid tendency in the taste of the time.

Line 2: the unstated subject of *langue* is Irene, the poet's beloved.

Line 5: *come...* begins a comparison of the dying woman to a flower, wilting in summer heat.

Line 8: *narciso* appears in the poem with the rare spelling *narcisso*.

Line 11: *puote* is a poetic form of the common verb *può*.

Line 16: *ordir* means to prepare a warp for weaving or, metaphorically, to plan or to sketch. The word implies that the gods would not know how to begin creating another Irene.

Musical Background

Although Verdi was rejected by the Conservatory in Milan—he was older than most beginners, came from too far away, and had faulty piano technique—he stayed in Milan and studied privately. In 1836 he received a contract from his hometown, Busseto, to teach in the local music school and conduct the town orchestra. He married soon after, and during nearly three years in Busseto he composed dozens of works for various vocal and instrumental forces. In 1838, while he was working on his first opera, *Oberto, Conte di San Bonifacio*, Verdi achieved his first publication, *Sei romanze* (6 Songs). In the same year the young couple's first child died. The tragic deaths of Verdi's other child and of his wife, Margherita, followed in the next two years.

For a full appreciation of Verdi's style, the student will want to hear recordings of great sopranos performing two arias that are closely related to this song. The arching phrase that begins in m25 is so powerfully expressive that Verdi adapted it to other uses in two of his greatest operas composed 15 years later. In *Il Trovatore* (The Troubadour, first produced in January, 1853), Leonora sings nearly the same phrase, in A-flat Major and with an enhanced harmonization, when she describes mysterious music that came to her through the night air. In *La Traviata* (The Woman Led Astray, first produced in March, 1853) Violetta sings a strikingly similar phrase when Alfredo appears at Flora's party at the end of Act II. Her words are, *"Ah, perché venni, incauta! Pietà, gran Dio, di me!"* (Ah, why did I come, incautious one! Pity on me, great God!). Violetta's melody, harmonized in F minor, rises one step higher than the similar phrase in this song; both phrases are despairing appeals for divine aid.

Although a first edition is usually a desirable source, it appears that Verdi made certain improvements in the second edition, published in Paris. He also changed the order of the six songs, placing this one first, perhaps because he decided that it was the best of them.

Sources

1) No. 1 in *6 Ariettes* (Paris: Pacini, no date), Milan (only two numbers). For voice and piano. Key: A-flat Major.

2) No. 3 in *Sei Romanze* (Milan: Gio. Canti, 1838), Ris. Mus. e.196-28, Milan. Dedication to Count Pietro Favagrossa. There is a pencilled notation made by musicologist Guglielmo Barblan in 1962: *"La prima edizione della prima opera di Verdi (1838). Unico esemplare conosciuto."* (The first edition of the first work of Verdi (1838). Only known copy.)

In solitaria stanza

Jacopo Vittorelli

Giuseppe Verdi
Edited by John Glenn Paton
(Range: E♭4–G♭5)

Lyrics under the staves:

In so-li-ta - ria stan - - za

lan - gue per do - glia a-tro - ce il lab - bro è sen - za

vo - ce, sen - za re-spi - ro il sen,_____

ⓐ "Walking movement." Suggested tempo: [quarter] = 80 - 88.

ⓑ The Milan edition indicates *mezza voce,* "half voice." Notice that the voice has dotted rhythms that contrast with triplets in the piano. If the 16th note is correctly sung after the last note of the triplet, there is a tension between the rhythms that adds great energy to the song. Verdi used this effect in many works.

ⓒ The slur over m4 denotes a smooth, expressive *legato.* (When a slur is over more than two notes, there is no *portamento.*) Obviously, the whole phrase is *legato,* but it was customary at this time to end most slurs at barlines. Similar situations are found in mm14 and 35. In later works, Verdi often wrote longer slurs that cannot even be sung in one breath.

ⓓ Verdi sindicated *portamenti* in mm7, 8, 10, 16, and 24-26. A *portamento* occurs when a slur connects two notes on different pitches that have two syllables of text. At the end of the first note the voice moves quickly to the pitch of the second note before changing to the second syllable. It was Vaccai's opinion (1834) that the voice should change the pitch cleanly, without sliding. Later in the 1800s the sliding *portamento* certainly became the standard.

Translation: In a lonely room she languishes in terrible pain; she cannot speak, she hardly breathes,

just like a tender narcissus that is dying in a deserted garden that is without dew under the summer heat.
Oppressed by anxiety,

21

cor - ro per vi - e ri - mɔ - te e

23

gri - - do in suɔn che puɔ - - te le

25

rallentando (e) *più mosso con enfasi* (f) *incalzando* (g)

ru - pi in-te - ne - rir: Sal - va-te͜o Dei pie -

rallentando *string.*

28

con grazia (h)

to - si, quel - la bel-tà ce - lɛ - ste! Voi

p

(e) A breath follows the *portamento*. That is, at the end of the first note, the voice moves up a whole step on the syllable *–rir*, and the singer breathes before singing *Sal-*.

(f) "With emphasis."

(g) "Growing warmer."

(h) "With grace."

I run through distant streets and cry out with a sound that would soften rocky cliffs: "Save her, o merciful gods, save that heavenly beauty! You

might never know how to create another as beautiful as she!"

ⓘ "Speeding up" in the voice and "With the singer" in the piano.

ⓙ "Held." Rather than a *fermata* on a single note, the *tenuto* slows down the whole measure. The upward accent marks imply strong emphasis, non-*legato*.

ⓚ "At pleasure," which always means slower.

Deh, pietoso, o Addolorata

[dɛ pjeto̱ːzo o‿ad̪ːdoloɾaːta]

Have Mercy, Oh Mother of Sorrows

Giuseppe Verdi (1813–1901)

dɛ   pjeto̱ːzo o ad̪ːdoloɾaːta
1. **Deh, pietoso, o Addolorata,**
Please, pitiful, oh sorrowful-woman,

kiːna̱ il   gwa̱rdo a̱l mi̱o dolo̱ːɾe
2. **China il   guardo al mio dolore.**
incline the gaze   to my sorrow.

tu uːna spaːda fit̪ːta̱ in ko̱ːɾe
3. **Tu, una spada fitta in core,**
You, a   sword fixed in heart,

vo̱ldʒi ʎːʎɔkːki dezolaːta
4. **Volgi gl'occhi, desolata,**
turn   the-eyes, desolate-one,

al   moɾɛnte tu̱o fiʎːʎwɔl
5. **Al   morente tuo figliuol.**
to-the dying   your son.

kwɛlːle̱ okːkjaːte̱ i   sospir vanːno
6. **Quelle occhiate e i sospir vanno**
Those   glances and the sighs are-going

lasːsu̱ al   paːdre son   pregjɛːɾa
7. **La sù   al   padre e son   preghiera**
there upward to-the Father and they-are prayer

ke̱il   suo tɛmpri̱ ed   il tu̱o afːfanːno
8. **Che il suo tempri   ed il tuo affanno.**
that the his he-may-mitigate and the your anxiety.

ko̱ːme̱ a̱ me skwartʃin   le viʃːʃeɾe
9. **Come a me squarcin   le viscere,**
How of me are-ripping-out the inner-organs,

ʎinsofːfɾiːbili mjɛi gwai
10. **Gl'insoffribili miei guai,**
the-insufferable my woes,

e delːlansjo pɛtːto̱ i   pa̱lpiti
11. **E dell'ansio   petto i   palpiti,**
and of-the-fearful bosom the tremors,

ki   kompɾɛndeɾe pwɔmːma̱i
12. **Chi comprendere può   mai?**
who understand can   ever?

di   ke trɛma̱ il   kɔr ke vwɔl
13. **Di   che trema il cor, che vuol,**
From what trembles the heart, what it-wants,

a tu so̱ːla il sa̱i tu sol
14. **Ah! tu sola, il sai   tu sol.**
ah, you only, it know you alone.

sɛmpre ovuŋkwe il pasːso̱ i̱o dʒiːɾo
15. **Sempre ovunque il   passo io giro**
Always, wherever the step   I turn,

kwal martiːɾo kwal martiːɾo
16. **Qual martiro, qual martiro!**
what suffering, what suffering

kwi nel sen   pɔrto kon me
17. **Qui nel sen   porto con me!**
here in-the bosom I-carry with me!

solitaːrjapːpeːna o   kwa̱nto
18. **Solitaria appena, oh quanto**
Alone   barely, oh, how much

vɛrso̱ alːloːɾa̱ o kwa̱nto   pja̱nto
19. **Verso allora, oh quanto   pianto,**
I pour then,   oh, how much weeping,

e   di   dɛntro skɔpːpja̱ il   kɔr
20. **E di   dentro scoppia il cor.**
and from within bursts-out the heart.

sul   vazɛl del   finestriːno
21. **Sul   vasel del   finestrino**
In-the vessel at-the little-window

la mi̱a laːkrima ʃendɛa
22. **La mia lacrima scendea**
the my tear   fell-down

kwando̱ alːlalba del   matːtiːno
23. **Quando all'alba del   mattino**
when   at-dawn of-the morning

kwesti fjor per te koʎːʎea
24. **Questi fior per te cogliea.**
these   flowers for you I-gathered.

ke del   soːle̱ il priːmo rad̪ːdʒo
25. **Che del   sole il primo raggio**
How of-the sun the first   ray

la mi̱a sta̱ntsa riskjaɾaːva
26. **La mia stanza rischiarava**
the my room   again-lighted

e   dal   lɛtːto mi katːtʃaːva
27. **E dal   letto mi cacciava**
and from-the bed me chased,

adʒitando̱mil   dolo̱r
28. **Agitandomi il dolor!**
agitating-in-me the sorrow!

a per te dal dizono̱ɾe
29. **Ah, per te dal disonore,**
Ah, by you from dishonor,

dalːla mɔrte̱ i̱o sia   salvaːta
30. **Dalla morte io sia   salvata.**
from death I may-be saved.

Poetic Background

"My beloved Saint, only you can help me. I am in grave danger of humiliation and even death."

The character is Gretchen in the play *Faust* by Johann Wolfgang von Goethe (1749–1832), who is revered as the greatest figure in German literature. *Faust*, published in its definitive form in 1808, is similarly regarded as a masterpiece of world literature.

The title character, Dr. Faust, is an aging philosopher who sells his soul to the Devil in return for a chance to be young again. As a handsome young man, he seduces the innocent Gretchen. In this scene Gretchen has just heard about another girl, who became pregnant and was abandoned by her lover. Now alone, Gretchen is overcome with guilt and fear, knowing that she is in danger of the same humiliation. Finding a little shrine that has been built into a niche in the city wall, she puts fresh flowers before an image of the Virgin Mary and pours out her heart in a prayer. (Later in the play Gretchen bears a baby, drowns it in an episode of insanity, and is imprisoned. When Faust comes to the prison to take her away, she is too weak and irrational to escape. As she dies, heavenly voices proclaim that she is saved, but the Devil takes Faust away.)

Verdi's music cannot be adapted to the original German text because the Italian text uses meters that are completely different from Goethe's. The translator was a friend of Verdi's from Busseto, Luigi Balestra (1808–1863).

Goethe's poem ends with a repetition of the first sentence, and Verdi changed the word order slightly so that the final emphasis is on the saint.

Line 1: *pietoso* modifies *guardo* in line 2. *Addolorata* is specifically the sorrowful Virgin Mary, contemplating the suffering of her son, Jesus Christ.

Line 3: Mary is sometimes portrayed with her heart exposed and a sword (or seven swords) piercing it.

Line 8: *il suo* and *il tuo* both modify *affanno*: "his (Jesus's) and your suffering." (*Affanno*, defined as "breathlessness" or as "anxiety," is often used as a synonym for "suffering.") The text setting seems awkward here, with a sustained note on *il*, but Italian style allows this.

Line 13 ends with a question mark in the first edition, but the thought continues to the next line.

Line 14: *il* refers to both uses of *che* in line 13: "*what* makes the heart tremble, *what* it wants, you know *it*."

Line 16: *martiro!* is the last punctuation in the printed song text until the period at the end. It has been necessary to speculate, consulting the German original, as to where sentences begin and end.

Line 18: *appena* means as soon as she is left alone.

Line 24: *cogliea* is a third person verb used to rhyme with line 22, but the only possible translation is in the first person.

Musical Background

For information about events in Verdi's life in 1838, please see the background to the previous song (page 00).

Franz Schubert began a musical setting of this scene, beginning *"Ach neige, du Schmerzenreiche,"* but he left it unfinished. The incomplete song was published in 1838, ten years after Schubert's death and, coincidentally, the same year when Verdi wrote his setting. The most famous musical version of the *Faust* story is Gounod's opera (1859), in which Gretchen's name is changed to Marguerite.

Source

No. 6 in *Sei Romanze* (Milan: Gio. Canti, no date), Ris. Mus. e.196-28, Milan. Poet identified as D[on?] Balestri. Dedication to Count Pietro Favagrossa. This copy bears a pencilled notation made by musicologist Guglielmo Barblan in 1962: *"La prima edizione della prima opera di Verdi (1838). Unico esemplare conosciuto."* (The first edition of the first work of Verdi (1838). Only known copy.) Key: F Minor.

Deh, pietoso, o Addolorata

Johann Wolfgang von Goethe
Translated by Luigi Balestra

Giuseppe Verdi
Edited by John Glenn Paton
(Range: C4–Gb5)

(a) Suggested tempo: ♩ = 62 – 68.

(b) Verdi indicated *portamenti* here and in mm9, 23, 27, etc. A *portamento* occurs when a slur connects two notes on different pitches that have two syllables of text. At the end of the first note the voice moves quickly to the pitch of the second note before changing to the second syllable. It was Vaccai's opinion (1834) that the voice should not slide between the two pitches but should make the pitch change cleanly. In Verdi's music the sliding *portamento* is probably expected, as it certainly was later in the 1800s.

Translation: Please, Mother of Sorrows, look with pity on my sorrow. With a sword piercing your heart, desolate,

la - ta, al mo - rɛn - te tuo fi - gliuɔl. Quel-le oc-

chia - te e i so - spir van - no la sù al pa - dre e son pre-

ghiɛ - ra che il suo tɛm - pri ed il tuo af - fan-no. Co - me a

ⓒ The slur over mm10–12 denotes a smooth, expressive *legato*. (When a slur is over more than two notes, there is no *portamento*.) The *legato* slurs over mm13–17 emphasize that the whole passage is one musical and poetic idea. Obviously, the singer needs to take one or more breaths, but the idea must be sustained. (Each slur lasts only one measure, but the meaning is the same as if there were one long slur, as Verdi usually wrote in later works.)

ⓓ If a breath is needed, the syllable –*dre* shortened and the conjunction *e* is omitted.

you are watching your dying Son. Your glances and sighs go up to the Father in a prayer to lessen his suffering and your own.

ⓔ "Moved." Suggested tempo: [quarter] = 98 – 110. The accents here and in m21 and strong emphases and, perhaps, not *legato*. The accents result in a stronger dynamic, which contrasts with the *piano* markings in mm20 and 22.

ⓕ *Portato*, the combination of a slur with dots, originated in violin music, where it means the articulation of several notes on one stroke of the bow, either up or down. Since the bow does not stop moving, the notes are lightly connected but are distinguished by variation in the pressure of the bow. A similar effect is wanted here: the tones are lightly connected but are made distinct by breath pressure.

My inner turmoil, my insufferable woes, the trembling of my bosom, who could understand them? Oh, you alone know why my heart beats,

ⓖ Suggested tempo: ♩ = 126 – 140.

ⓗ Suggested tempo: ♩ = 92 – 100.

what it desires! Always, wherever I walk, what agony I am carrying in my breast! As soon as I am alone, how much

① Suggested tempo: ♩ = 82–90.

weeping pours out, as if my heart is bursting. My tears fell on the flower-box at dawn this morning when I gathered

52

ti - no que-sti fior per te co - glie - a. Che del

55

stringendo un pocoⓙ

so - le il pri - mo rag - gio la mia stan - za ri - schia -

58

con forza ⓚ

ra - va e dal let - to mi ___ cac - cia - va, a - gi -

61

tan - do - mi il do - lor. Ah, per te ___ dal di - so -

ⓙ "Quicken a little." Suggestions: Increase the tempo so that the scales in m59 are exciting. Keep the quicker tempo through the word *agitandomi*. Extend the syllable *–mi* with a *fermata*. In m62 resume the same tempo as at m47.

ⓚ "Forcefully."

flowers for you. How the first rays of the sun brightened my room and drove me from my bed, awakening my sorrow. Ah, may I be saved by you from dishonor

no - re, dal - la mor - te io sia sal - va - ta. Dεh, pie-

to - so, al mio do - lo - re, chi - na il

allargando ①

allargando

mancando ⓜ

guar - do o Ad-do-lo - ra - ta.

p

morendo

① Suggestion: Slow the tempo to *adagio*, as at the beginning of the song.
ⓜ "Fainting."

and from death!

Il Bacio
The Kiss

Luigi Arditi (1822–1903)
[luiːdʒi ardiːti]

sulːle labːbra se potesːsi
1. **Sulle   labbra, se potessi,**
On-the lips,   if I-could,

doltʃe un baːtʃo ti   darɛi
2. **Dolce   un bacio ti   darei.**
sweet a kiss   to-you I-would-give.

tutːte tutːte ti   dirɛi
3. **Tutte, tutte ti   direi**
All, all   to-you I-would-say

le doltʃetːtse delːlamoːr
4. **Le dolcezze   dell'amor.**
the sweetnesses of-love.

sɛmpre asːsiza te dapːprɛsːso
5. **Sempre assisa a te d'appresso,**
Always seated by you beside,

milːle gaudiː ti   dirɛi
6. **Mille   gaudii ti   direi.**
thousand joys   to-you I-would-say,

ed i palpiti   udirɛi
7. **Ed i palpiti   udirei**
and the palpitations I-would-hear

ke rispondono al mio kɔr
8. **Che rispondono al mio cor.**
that answer   to my heart.

dʒɛmːme e   pɛrle non deziːo
9. **Gemme   e   perle non desio,**
Gems   and pearls not I-desire,

non son vaːga daltro afːfɛtːto
10. **Non son vaga   d'altro affetto;**
Not I-am desirous of-other affection;

un tuo zgwardo ɛ il miːo dilɛtːto
11. **Un tuo sguardo è il mio diletto,**
a your glance   is the my   delight,

un tuo baːtʃo ɛ il mio tezɔr
12. **Un tuo bacio è il mio tesor.**
a your kiss   is the my treasure.

vjeːni a vjɛn pju non tardarə
13. **Vieni, ah, vien! più   non tardare.**
Come, ah, come! More not delay.

vjeːni a vjeni a me dapːprɛsːso
14. **Vieni, ah, vieni a me d'appresso,**
Come, ah, come to me close,

nelːlebːbretːtsa dunamplɛsːso
15. **Nell'ebbrezza   d'un amplesso**
In-the-exhilaration of-an embrace,

kio   viːva sol damoːr
16. **Ch'io   viva sol d'amor.**
so-that-I may-live only from-love.

Poetic Background

"I want to enjoy all the pleasures of love with you."

Gottardo Aldighieri (1824–1906) had a good reputation as a high baritone. Line 1: *Sulle* and other words are broken. The first syllable is sung as *su-*, not as *sul-*. All other broken words are treated in this fashion; that is, the syllable ends with a vowel and the consonant is sung on the next note..

Musical Background

In autumn 1859 Arditi and his wife Virginia were in Manchester, England, touring with a troupe of Italian singers. One of them was Marietta Piccolòmini (1834–1899), a brilliant soprano who had sung both the London and Paris premieres of Verdi's *La Traviata*. While playing in the hotel lobby after dinner, Arditi improvised a waltz melody that charmed Piccolòmini, and he wrote it down at her urging. When she left for several months of touring in America, she exacted a promise that Arditi would compose a new song for her next concert in England. When the date was drawing near, he remembered the slip of paper with the waltz tune and began to develop the tune into an extended song. This is the story of the words as told by Arditi in *My Reminiscences*:

"A high baritone, of the name of Aldighieri, and a very excellent singer to boot, was practising with me one morning, and I told him that I was greatly in need of words for my song.

" 'I will write you some verses if you will give me an idea,' he answered promptly. 'What subject would you like?'

"Virginia, who was sewing at the other end of the room, answered ere I had time to think of anything, and said: 'Why not write about a kiss? There's a good subject for you!'

"Aldighieri thought the idea an excellent one, and forthwith set to work and wrote the words to *"Il Bacio,"* which have since become famous."

Piccolòmini received the song on the day before her concert at the seaside resort of Brighton, but she learned it in a few hours and performed it with success.

Arditi sold *"Il Bacio"* and three other pieces to the London publisher J. B. Cramer for ?50. Years later he heard that the copyright had changed hands for ?640, but he never made any further money from the international hit.

Arditi used many articulation signs in this song, perhaps influenced by Piccolomini's vivacious style. Upward accents appear with *staccato* dots (m25), without dots (m29) and under a slur (m31). Horizontal accents appear on the attack of a held note (m41) and under a slur (m63). M43 has a *staccato* shaped like a teardrop or wedge (pointed up or down according to the position of the note), and in m133, beat 3, there are two accents on the same note (by mistake?). It is no longer possible to define all these articulations precisely, but they reflect a varied and energetic performance in keeping with the lively tempo.

Notice that at m179, the first melody reappears in *pp*, but with none of the accent marks that were present at the beginning.

Approaching the climax, Arditi borrows a device from *"Sempre libera"* in *La Traviata* (1852): in measures 231-234 the vowel of *ah!* is rearticulated, but no breaths are taken between the notes.

Source

"Il Bacio, valzer brillante" (Milan: G. Ricordi, 1861, first Italian edition), B-35-h-225-7/VI, Milan. Key: D Major.

Il Bacio

Gottardo Aldighieri

Luigi Arditi
(Range: C#4–B5)

Tempo di Valse. Allegro brillante ⓐ

ⓐ Suggested tempo: ♩. = 66–72

ⓑ "With much soul and brilliance, and well marked (stressed)." Observe the rest that interrupts sul- le and several other words. This artistic representation of agitated sighing is called by the Latin term suspiratio in the art of rhetoric. Examples are found in arias by Mozart ("Smanie implacabili" from Così fan tutte) and Verdi ("Caro nome" from Rigoletto) and in several other songs in this volume.

Translation: If I could, I would give you a sweet kiss on your lips. I would say to you all the sweet words of love.

ⓒ The slur that extends through m49-50 shows that the musical thought continues even though the sound is interrupted. It is preferable not to breathe during the rest. This also occurs in mm124, 132, etc.

ⓓ Arditi indicated a portamento (also in mm64, 76, 84 and elsewhere), which occurs when a slur connects two notes on different pitches that have two syllables of text. At the end of the first note the voice moves quickly to the pitch of the second note before changing to the second syllable. Vaccai (1834) said that the voice should change the pitch cleanly, without sliding, but Arditi probably expected sliding portamenti, which became standard in the later 1800s.

Always sitting beside you, I would tell you a thousand happy things

ⓔ Portato, the combination of a slur with dots, originated in violin music, where it means the articulation of several notes on one stroke of the bow, either up or down. Since the bow does not stop moving, the notes are lightly connected but are distinguished by variation in the pressure of the bow. A similar effect is wanted here: the tones are lightly connected but are made distinct by breath pressure.

and I would feel your heart beating like mine. Gems and pearls are not my wish, nor

son va - ga—d'al - tro af - fɛt - to;

con tutta forza

un———— tuo sguar - do è il mi - o di - let - to, un tuo

do I want any other love:

ⓕ Arditi indicated flute, oboe, and clarinet for the staccato chords and trumpets entering in m151. These are remnants of the original orchestration.

your kiss is my treasure. Come, ah, come, without delay.

Come, ah come to me so that, in the exhilaration of an embrace, I am living solely from love.

Dimenticar, ben mio

/dimentikar bɛn mio/

How Could You Forget?

Amilcare Ponchielli (1834–1886)
[amilkaːre poŋkjɛlːli]

dimentikar bɛn mio koːme ai potuːto
1. **Dimenticar, ben mio, come hai potuto**
To-forget, good mine, how were-you able

ke il tuo kɔr tanto tɛmpo ɔ posːseduːto
2. **Che il tuo cor tanto tempo ho posseduto?**
that the your heart so-much time I-have possessed?

kwel kɔr si falso e kaːro oːve trovaːre
3. **Quel cor si falso e caro! Ove trovare**
That heart so false and dear! Where to-find

kɔːze ke sien pju false e insjɛm pju kaːre
4. **Cose che sien più false e insiem più care?**
things that would-be more false and also more dear?

koːme ai lamoːre il dwoːlo dimentikaːto
5. **Come hai l'amore e il duolo dimenticato**
How have-you he-love and the-sorrow forgotten,

ke tanto tɛmpo il kɔr manːno stratːtsjaːto
6. **Che tanto tempo il cor m'hanno straziato?**
that so-much time my heart have tortured?

io non saprɛi dei duːe kwal fu il madːdʒor
7. **Io non saprei dei due qual fu il maggior:**
I not would-know of-the two which was the greater:

sɔ ke grande fu il dwoːlo grande lamoːr
8. **So che grande fu il duolo, grande l'amor!**
I-know that great was the sorrow, great the-love!

Poetic Background

"I'm shocked that you could forget the great love I had for you."
Ponchielli translated the poem from one by Heinrich Heine.
The dominant theme of Heine's poetry was his resentment because a cousin whom he loved married another man.

Peter W. Shea of the University of Massachusetts at Amherst identified the poem as No. 21 of Heine's *Lyrisches Intermezzo*.

The German text is:

So hast du ganz und gar vergessen,
Daß ich so lang dein Herz besessen,
Dein Herzchen so süß und so falsch und so klein,
Es kann nirgend was Süß'res und Falscheres sein.

So hast du die Lieb' und das Leid vergessen,
Die das Herz mir täten zusammenpressen.
Ich weiß nicht, war Liebe größer als Leid?
Ich weiß nur, sie waren groß allebeid'!

Line 3: *Ove* is a poetic form of *dove*. *Trovare*, an infinitive, is used with the main verb understood: "Where could one find...?"

Line 4: *sieno* is an obsolete subjunctive form of *essere*, now replaced by *siano*.

Musical Background

Ponchielli's song exemplifies the grandiose, highly dramatic style of the late Romantic era, found also in his operas. Beginning quietly, the two stanzas of the song build to a powerful climax that contrasts the minor key of *duolo* with the major key of *amor*. The final statement of *l'amore* leaves the voice unaccompanied to make its heartfelt statement and completely justifies the passionate piano postlude.

A noticeable characteristic of this style is the frequent use of long phrase marks to reinforce the general concept of legato. When phrase marks extend across an obvious place where the singer must take a breath (see m27), they serve as a reminder that the emotional energy of the phrase is continuous.

Ponchielli habitually wrote for powerful voices in both operas and songs. He was married to Teresina Brambilla, who was the niece and student of Marietta Brambilla, also a famous singer and the composer of a song in this volume. Teresina was the choice of both Ponchielli and Verdi to sing dramatic soprano roles.

Another song by Ponchielli, "*L'Eco*," is found in *Italian Art Songs of the Romantic Era*, edited by Patricia Adkins Chiti (Alfred Publishing Co.) along with portraits of the composer and his wife. "*L'Eco*" is also a setting of a poem translated from Heine.

Source

"*Dimenticar ben mio, romanza*" (Milan: Emilio Ribolzi, undated), editor's personal collection. (There were later editions by Pigna, 1900, and Ricordi, ca. 1901.) Dedication "*all'amico Gio. Rinaldi*." Original key: Bb Major.

Dimenticar, ben mio

From the German of Heinrich Heine
Translated by the composer

Amilcare Ponchielli
Edited by John Glenn Paton
(Range: F4–G5)

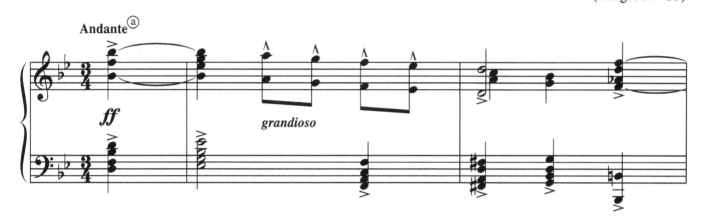

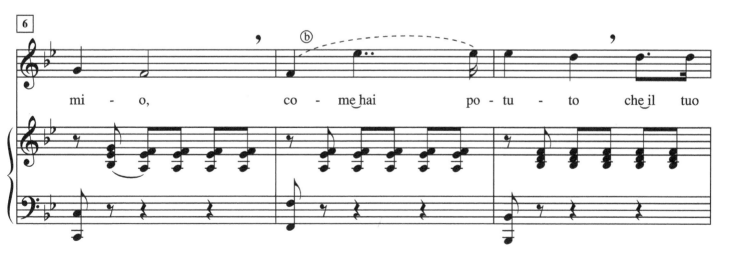

ⓐ Suggested tempo: ♩ = 69–76

ⓑ Because of the wide leap, one might sing *-me* as a grace note, on the lower pitch, with *hai* on beat 2. It is usually wrong to add a note in this way, but the diphthong *–me hai* occurring on a sudden leap would sound awkward.

Translation: How could you forget, my dear, that for so long I have possessed your

cor   tan - to tɛm - po hɔ pos - se - du -

to?   Quel cɔr   si fal - so,   si

fal -   so e ca - ro! O - ve tro - va - re

cɔ - se che sien più fal - se e in-siɛm più ca - re?

ⓒ The grace notes should probably be sung ahead of beat 3 on the syllable *pos-*. (The slur is missing in the source.)

ⓓ The half-step portamento gives a significant inflection to the word *false*, as it does in m34 to *duolo*. A wider portamento is in m28, just before the phrase "have tormented me."

heart? That heart so false and dear! that contains things that are so false and dear?

ⓔ The meaning of the text from m24-29 permits a breath in only two places, after *dimenticato* and after the first *cor*. In m25 a breath is taken quickly or not at all. In m27 a breath is taken dramatically, with strong emotional emphasis on the second *cor*. Possibly, there could be an upward *portamento* sung on the first *cor*, before the breath. The composer's phrase markings over m25 and m27 indicate that the singer must keep the emotional continuity of the long phrase.

ⓕ "More quickly, with warmth."

How have you forgotten the love and sorrow that tortured me for so long? I do not know which of the two was greater: I know that the sorrow was great, that the

gran - de fu il duɔ - lo, Sɔ che gran - de fu il
duɔ - lo. Gran - de l'a - mor, Gran -
de l'a - l'a - l'a - mo - re!

ⓖ *A tempo* here is slower than the preceding *animato*. "Expanding" is an unusual instruction and probably means to slow the tempo. The chords in the piano are marked "heavy."

ⓗ *Tenuto*, held, is used to make a note longer, but less than a *fermata*. It is understood to lengthen all of the notes in the measure.

love was great!

Donna, vorrei morir

/dɔnːna vorːrɛi moɾir/

Lady, I Would Die

Francesco Paolo Tosti (1846–1908)

/frantʃesko paolo tɔsti/

dɔnːna vorːrɛi   moɾir ma konfortaːto
1. **Donna, vorrei   morir, ma confortato**
   Lady, I-would-like to-die, but comforted

dalːlonɛsto   tuo amor
2. **Dall'onesto   tuo amor;**
   by-the-sincere your love,

sentiɾmi almeːno   uːna sol   vɔltaːmaːto
3. **Sentirmi   almeno una sol   volta amato**
   to-feel-myself at-least one single time loved

sɛntsaveɾne   rosːsoɾ
4. **Senza averne   rossor.**
   without having-from-it blushing.

vorːrɛi   potɛrti   dar   kwel pɔ ke rɛsta
5. **Vorrei   poterti   dar   quel po' che resta**
   I-would-like to-be-able-to-you to-give that little that remains

delːla mia dʒoventu
6. **Della mia gioventù;**
   of   my youth,

sovra lɔmeɾo   tuo pjegaɾ la tɛsta
7. **Sovra l'omero   tuo piegar la testa**
   upon the-shoulder yours to-bend the head

e   non destaɾmi   pju
8. **E   non destarmi   più.**
   and not to-wake-myself more.

Poetic Background

"If you loved me, even for a short time, I would need nothing else in this life."

Olindo Guerrini (1845–1916) published his works under several pseudonyms, including "Lorenzo Stecchetti." To add pathos to his poems, Guerrini invented a biography for "Stecchetti," supposedly his cousin and best friend, who died of tuberculosis at the age of 31. The poems first appeared in *Postuma* (Posthumous, Bologna: Zanichelli, 1877), accompanied by a photograph supposed to represent the poet. The poems were tremendously popular and prominent composers set them to music. *Postuma* went through 32 editions during Guerrini's lifetime.

The story of "Stecchetti" gives poignancy to the phrase, "the little that is left of my youth." His desperate situation is skillfully expressed in a simple, classical form: eight rhymed lines that alternate eleven and seven syllables (truncated).

Ruggero Leoncavallo also set this poem to music.

Line 4: *rossor* signifies shame because the poet's love is rejected.

Musical Background

At the age of 20 Tosti received a diploma from the Conservatory at Naples and returned home to Ortona. He was in poor health and went through periods of disillusionment, but he also organized and directed a small opera company to present operas by Donizetti and Verdi. Ortona temporarily became prosperous through the building of a railway along the Adriatic, but in 1869 the railway was completed and the support of Tosti's opera theater disappeared. He moved to Ancona, also on the Adriatic coast, and gave singing lessons there.

In 1870 Tosti moved to Rome where he was successful as a performer of his own songs. By the time he read *Postuma*, he was spending a great deal of time in London, where he eventually established himself for a large part of his career.

The first dated edition of *"Donna, vorrei morir"* is the source listed below. There is, however, a printed copy at the Biblioteca Giorgio Cini, Venice, that lacks a publisher's name. It may be Tosti's attempt at self-publishing before his contact with Ricordi.

Source

No. 3 in *Pagine d'album* (Album Pages) (Milano: Ricordi, 1880). Published in three keys: E, D and C Minor.

Donna, vorrei morir

Olindo Guerrini (Lorenzo Stecchetti)

Francesco Paolo Tosti
Edited by John Glenn Paton
(Range: F♯4–G♯5)

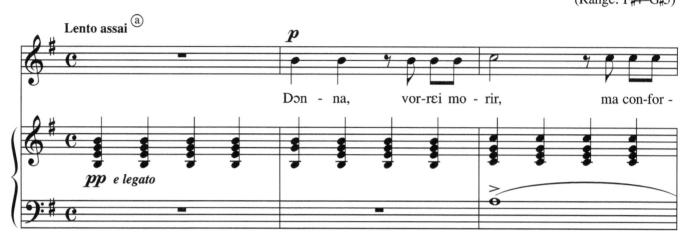

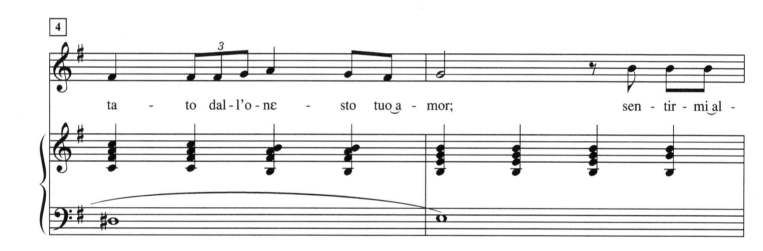

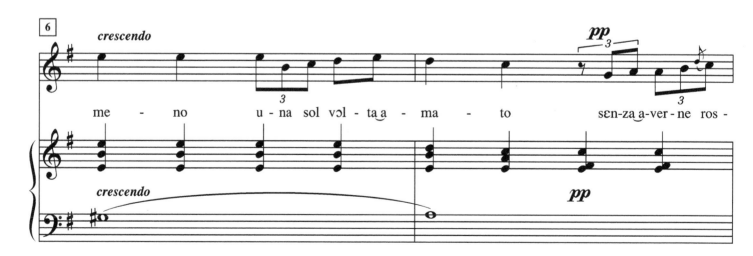

ⓐ "Very slow." Suggested tempo: ♩. = 42–46.

Translation: My lady, I would like to die, but die comforted by your sincere love; I would like to feel, at least just once, loved without shame.

I would like to give you the little that is left of my youth, to rest my head on your shoulder and never wake up again.

Ideale
/idea:le/

Ideal

Francesco Paolo Tosti (1846–1908)

io ti segwi: ko:mi:ride di pa:tʃe
1. **Io ti seguii com'iride di pace**
I you followed like rainbow of peace

luŋgo le vi:e del tʃɛ:lo
2. **Lungo le vie del cielo:**
along the ways of heaven:

io ti segwi: ko:me unami:ka fa:tʃe
3. **Io ti seguii come un'amica face**
I you followed like a friendly light

de:la nɔt:te nel ve:lo
4. **De la notte nel velo.**
of the night in-the veil.

e ti senti: nel:la lu:tʃe nel:la:rja
5. **E ti sentii ne la luce, ne l'aria,**
And you I-felt in the light, in the air,

nel profu:mo dei fjɔ:ri
6. **Nel profumo dei fiori;**
in-the perfume of-the flowers,

e fu pjɛ:na la stantsa solita:rja
7. **E fu piena la stanza solitaria**
and was full the room solitary

di te dei twɔi splendo:ri
8. **Di te, dei tuoi splendori.**
of you, of your splendors!

in te rapi:to al swɔn de:la tua vɔ:tʃe
9. **In te rapito, al suon de la tua voce,**
In you caught-up, at-the sound of — your voice,

luŋgamente so:ɲai
10. **Lungamente sognai;**
at-length I-dreamed;

e de:la tɛr:ra oɲ:ɲaf:fan:no oɲ:ɲi krɔ:tʃe
11. **E de la terra ogni affanno, ogni croce,**
and of the earth every grief, every cross,

in kwel soɲ:ɲo skordai
12. **In quel sogno scordai.**
you-will-be-in-the-air around at-the blackhair!

tɔrna ka:ro ideal tɔrna un istante
13. **Torna, caro ideal, torna un istante**
Return, dear ideal, return an instant

a sor:ridermi aŋkɔ:ra
14. **A sorridermi ancora,**
to smile-at-me again,

e a me risplendera nel tuo sembjante
15. **E a me risplenderà, nel tuo sembiante,**
and to me will-shine-again in your face

una novel:lauro:ra
16. **Una novell'aurora.**
a new dawn.

Poetic Background

"Your light filled my life, which is empty without it. Come back, dear ideal."

Carmelo Errico (1848–1892) also wrote the text of Tosti's *"Ave Maria."* A collection of his poems was reprinted in 1979. The poem is in four stanzas and has the classical form of alternating lines of eleven and seven syllables, with every line rhymed.

Line 12: Tosti mistakenly changed *sogno* to *giorno* (day).

Musical Background

At first hearing it seems that this song will have two identical stanzas. But the stanzas are subtly different in rhythm to accommodate the slight differences in word rhythms; compare especially m9 with m26 to see how effectively Tosti does this. Also, when the second stanza is at the midpoint (m29), a magically new sound arrives with the word *"Torna"*; in the original key it would be a supertonic triad, but it is ambiguous and does not resolve

in an expected way. This simple but mysterious chord is heard only once; when the melody repeats in m31, the bass note is changed. It is an effect that one might expect from Brahms, who also liked to lead the second stanza of a song in an unforeseeable direction. If the singer and pianist are both aware of this inspired moment, they can truly reach the listener's heart.

The male soprano Alessandro Moreschi (1858–1922) made a fascinating recording of this song. He was the last *castrato* singer employed by the Vatican. He recorded the song in April 1902 in the presence of his fellow choristers, who can be heard cheering for him at the end.

Source

"Ideale, melodia" (Milano: Ricordi, undated [1882]). Dedication to Mr. Jules Devaux. Published in three keys: A, G and F major.

Ideale

Francesco Paolo Tosti
Edited by John Glenn Paton
(Range: E4–F♯5)

Carmelo Errico

Io ti se - guii____ co - m'i - ri - de di

pa - ce lun - go le vie del ciɛ - lo: io ti se -

ⓐ Metronome marking from the composer.　　ⓑ Both here and in m9, the second *–i* of *seguii* receives a slight, but audible breath impulse on beat 2.

Translation: I followed you as if you were a rainbow of peace on the way to heaven; I followed you

© "Col canto" (with the voice) always implies that the singer is free to stretch the tempo, whether or not there is a marking in the voice part. The tempo returns to normal in the next measure.

as if you were a torch lighting the canopy of night. And I felt you in the light, in the air, in the scent of flowers; my lonely room was full of you and of your splendor.

ⓓ Here and in m27, the final *–i* is sung on beat 2.

Caught up in you, in the sound of your voice, I dreamed a long time, and in that

dream I forgot every worry, every burden of the world. Come back, my dear ideal, come back for a instant to smile at me again, and in your face

a new dawn will shine out.

Mattinata
/maːtːinaːta/
Morning Song

Ruggero Leoncavallo (1857–1919)
/ruːdːdʒɛːro leoŋkavalːlo/

lauroːra di bjaŋko vestiːta
1. L'aurora di bianco vestita
The-dawn in white   clothed

dʒa   luʃːʃo diskjuːde al   gran sol
2. Già   l'uscio dischiude al   gran sol,
already the-door opens   to-the great sun,

di   dʒa   kon le roze: sue diːta
3. Dì già   con le rosee sue dita
Day already with the pink its   fingers

karetːtsa de fjoːri lo stwɔl
4. Carezza de' fiori   lo stuol!
caresses   of flowers the crowd!

komːmɔsːso da un frɛːmito arkaːno
5. Commosso da un fremito arcano
Moved   by a shudder mysterious

intorno il   kreaːto dʒa   par
6. Intorno il   creato già   par,
all-around the creation already seems,

e tu non ti   dɛsti edinvaːno
7. E tu non ti   desti, ed invano
and you not yourself waken, and in-vain

mi stɔ kwi dolɛnte a kantar
8. Mi sto   qui dolente a cantar:
I stand here sad   to sing:

metːti aŋke tu la vɛste bjaŋka
9. Metti anche tu la veste bianca
Put-on also   you the dress white

e   skjuːdi luʃːʃo al tuo kantor
10. E   schiudi l'uscio al tuo cantor!
and open   the-door to your singer!

oːve non sɛi   la luːtʃe maŋka
11. Ove non sei   la luce   manca,
Where not you-are the light is-missing,

oːve tu sɛi naʃːʃe lamor
12. Ove tu sei nasce l'amor!
where you are is-born love!

Poetic Background

"Come and see the beautiful morning. The only thing it lacks is you."

Leoncavallo preferred to set his own poems to music, including the libretto to his only successful opera, *Pagliacci.*

Title: a *mattinata* is a song sung to wake up a beloved lady.

Line 3: *rosee* does not mean roses; it is an adjective, "pink," with a feminine plural ending. *Dita* is an irregular feminine plural to *dito* (masculine), "finger."

Musical Background

Leoncavallo, a business-minded and forward thinking man, watched developments in the recording of sound. His *"Mattinata"* was "written expressly for the gramophone" (*"scritta espressamente pel Grammofono"*), as the cover of the first edition proudly announced. The greatest tenor of the time, Enrico Caruso, recorded the song in April 1904 with the composer at the piano. It immediately became a popular classic. Innumerable great singers have performed and recorded it, often with the last five notes transposed up an octave.

Although the text has a male viewpoint, the high version of the first edition is labeled "for tenor or soprano."

Leoncavallo's given name, Ruggero, was also spelled Ruggiero in his lifetime. The poet Gabriele d'Annunzio pointed out that Leoncavallo's name "combined two noble beasts," the lion and the horse.

Source

"Mattinata" (Milan: Gramophone Co., 1904 [later assigned to G. Ricordi]). Dedication to Teresa Arkel. Published in three keys: E, D and C Major.

Mattinata
Ruggero Leoncavallo

Ruggero Leoncavallo
Edited by John Glenn Paton
(Range: C#4–G#5)

ⓐ Suggested tempo: ♪ = 112 – 124. "Sonorously."

Translation: Dawn, dressed in white, is opening the door to the great sun; Day is already caressing the host of flowers with her rosy fingers!

stuɔl!_____ Com-mɔs-so da un frɛ - mi - to ar-ca - no   in-

tor-no il cre - a - to   già par,_____   e   tu non   ti de - sti,   ed in-

va - no   mi stɔ qui do-lɛn-te a   can - tar:

ⓑ All phrasings in this song, both slurs and breath marks, come from the composer.

ⓒ Leoncavallo indicated the *portamento*, which occurs when a slur connects two different pitches that have two syllables of text. At the end of the first note the voice slides to the pitch of the second note before changing to the second syllable. There is also a *portamento* at the climax of the song in m28.

All of creation seems to be moved by a mysterious trembling—and you have not awakened,
and I am standing here sadly to sing:

ⓓ The double grace note is sung with the syllable *ve-* ahead of the beat, taking time from the previous note.

"Put on your white dress, too, and open the door for your singer! Wherever you are not, there is no light; wherever you are, love is born!"

Lasciati amar
[laʃːʃati amaːr]

Let Me Love You

Ruggero Leoncavallo (1857–1919)

forse in fondo al tuo kɔːre
1. **Forse in fondo al tuo core**
Maybe in bottom of your heart

non loːnegar
2. **(Non lo negar!),**
(do-not it deny!),

kɔːme un radːdʒo damoːre
3. **Come un raggio d'amore,**
like a ray of-love,

staː per spuntar
4. **Sta per spuntar.**
is about-to dawn.

ɛ un mɔːto straːno
5. **È un moto strano,**
It-is an emotion strange,

un sɛnso arkaːno
6. **Un senso arcano,**
a sense mysterious,

ke unːnwɔːvo palpito fa in te vibrar
7. **Che un nuovo palpito fa in te vibrar!**
which a new trembling makes in you vibrate!

kɔːme unalba novɛlːla
8. **Come un'alba novella**
As a-dawn new

surdʒe per te
9. **Surge per te,**
Rises for you,

tutːto intorno sabːbɛlːla
10. **Tutto intorno s'abbella**
everything around itself-beautifies,

ne sai perke
11. **né sai perché!**
nor do-you-know why!

tutːto ɛ fjoriːto
12. **Tutto è fiorito,**
All is in-flower,

e il kɔr zmarːriːto
13. **È il cor smarrito**
and the heart bewildered

non sa se gaudjoːdwɔːlo eʎːʎɛ
14. **Non sa se gaudio o duolo egli è.**
not knows if rejoicing or sorrow it is.

dal soɲːɲo tuo novɛlːlo
15. **Dal sogno tuo novello**
By-the dream your new

laʃːʃatialfin kulːlar
16. **Lasciati alfin cullar,**
let-yourself finally be-cradled;

skjuːdi le bratːtʃa
17. **Schiudi le braccia**
open the arms

damoːre in tratːtʃa
18. **D'amore in traccia,**
of-love in sign;

lamore ɛ bɛlːlo laʃːʃa ti amar
19. **L'amore è bello, lasciati amar!**
Love is beautiful, let - yourself be-loved!

Poetic Background

"Look around you at the beauty of Nature, and open yourself up to my love."

Leoncavallo usually set his own poems to music, as he did also in *"Mattinata."* Both songs associate a beautiful morning with the discovery of love.

Line 4: *sta per* means "is about to." The verb has no stated subject; "something" is about to arise.

Line 18: *traccia* means "trail" in the sense of the tracks and signs left behind by an animal. The word is chosen to rhyme with *braccia*. Possible meaning: "Open your arms as a sign of love."

Line 19: *lasciati* is changed to *ti lascia* on the repetition (m49) to provide an open vowel for the high note.

Musical Background

Leoncavallo had his greatest success at age 35 with *Pagliacci*. He composed many promising works after that, but none of his operas reached the same level of public acclaim. His reputation was international and some of his works were more popular in Germany than in Italy. In 1912 he wrote an opera for London, *Zingari* (Gypsies), and the Lyric Opera of Chicago commissioned him to write a major work that remained unfinished when he died.

Leoncavallo wrote many instructions for interpretation, and their meanings are found in the list of musical terms on page 000.

The source used here is the first North American edition. The song had been published in 1913 by Carlo Schmidl in Trieste.

Source

"Come, Love Divine; Lasciati amar" (New York: M. Witmark, 1915). English words by Wm. H. Gardner. "Written for, dedicated to and sung by Mr. Enrico Caruso." Published in three keys: E♭, C and B♭ Major.

Lasciati amar

Ruggero Leoncavallo

Ruggero Leoncavallo
Edited by John Glenn Paton
(Range: E♭4–A♭5, small head B♭5)

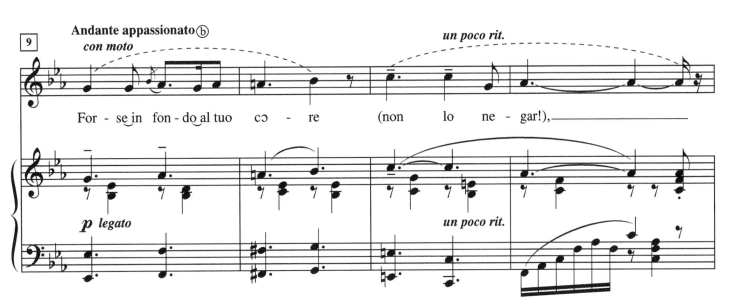

Forse in fondo al tuo core (non lo negar!),

ⓐ "Broadly," with great flexibility in the introduction.

ⓑ "Slowly, passionately," suggested tempo: [eighth] = 92 – 100, with attention to all of the indicated variations in tempo. Grace notes are all ahead of the beat, taking time from the preceding rest or note. Phrasing and breath marks are from the composer.

Translation: Perhaps deep in your heart (don't deny it!)

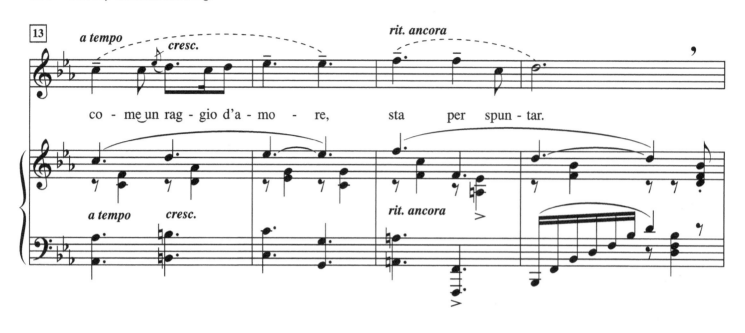

co - me un rag - gio d'a - mo - re, sta per spun - tar.

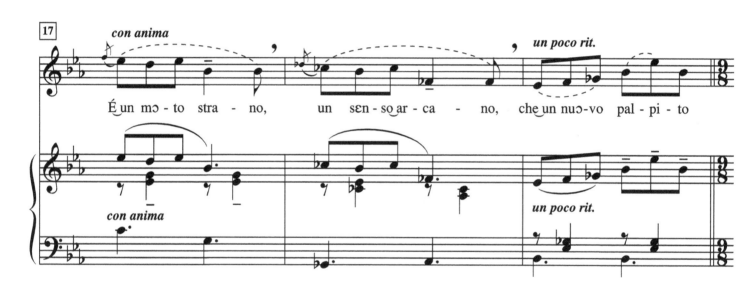

É un mɔ - to stra - no, un sɛn - so ar - ca - no, che un nuɔ - vo pal - pi - to

fa in te vi - brar!_____ Co - me u - n'al - ba no - vɛl - la___ sur - ge per

a ray of love is about to shine. It is a strange emotion, a mysterious sense, that makes a new trembling vibrate in you.
As a new dawn rises for you,

te,_____ tut - to in - tor - no s'ab - bɛl - la,   né   sai   per -

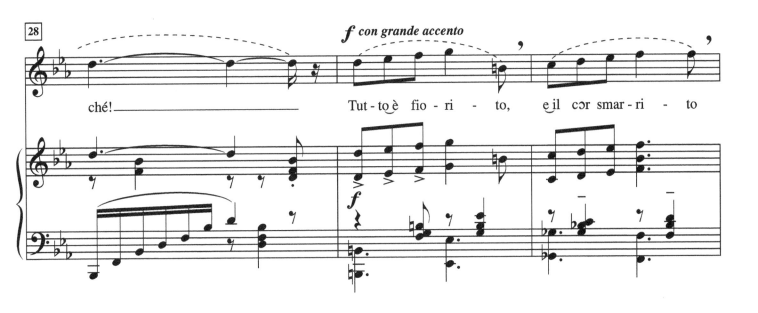

ché!_____   Tut - to è fio - ri - to,   e il cɔr smar - ri - to

non sa se gau - dio o duɔ - lo e - gli è._____

everything around you becomes beautiful, and you don't know why!

Dal so - gno tuo no - vɛl - lo

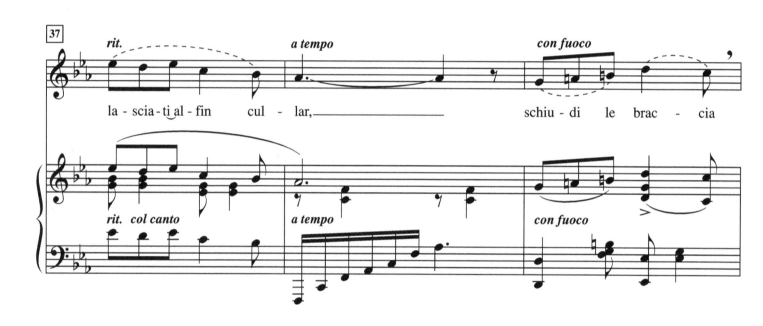

la - scia - ti_al - fin cul - lar,_____ schiu - di le brac - cia

d'a - mo - rɛ_in trac - cia, l'a - mo - rɛ_è bɛl - lo, la - scia - ti_a - mar!_____

Rest in the cradle of your new dream; open your arms to love. Love is beautiful, let yourself be loved!

43 con affetto ritenuto   a tempo   poco stentato

Dal so-gno tuo no-vɛl - lo_____ la-scia-ti al-fin cul-

46 riprendendo con fuoco   tenuto

lar,_____ schiu-di le brac - cia d'a-mo-re in trac - cia, l'a-mo-re è

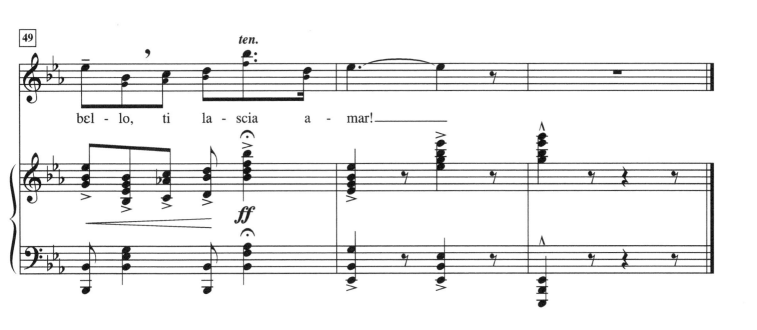

49 ten.

bɛl-lo, ti la-scia a-mar!_____

Sole e Amore

/soːle amoːre/

Sun and Love

Giacomo Puccini (1858–1924)
/dʒaːkomo putːtʃiːni/

il soːle alːlegramente
1. **Il sole allegramente**
The sun cheerfully

batːte ai twɔi veːtri amor
2. **Batte ai tuoi vetri. Amor**
knocks at your windows. Love

pjan pjan batːte al tuo kwɔre
3. **Pian pian batte al tuo cuore,**
softly softly knocks at your heart,

e luːno e laltro kjaːma
4. **E l'uno e l'altro chiama.**
and one and the-other calls.

il soːle diːtʃe o dormente
5. **Il sole dice: O dormente,**
The sun says, "O sleeping-one,

mostrati ke sɛi bɛlːla
6. **Mostrati che sei bella.**
show-yourself, how you-are beautiful."

diːtʃe lamor sorɛlːla
7. **Dice l'amor: Sorella,**
Says love: "Sister,

kol tuo priːmo pensjɛr pɛnsa ki taːma
8. **Col tuo primo pensier pensa a chi t'ama!**
with your first thought, think of one-who you-loves!"

al paganiːni dʒi putːʃiːni
9. **(Al Paganini. G. Puccini.)**
(To-the Paganini. G. Puccini.)

Poetic Background

"Come and see the beautiful morning. The only thing it lacks is you."

Although it is not called a *mattinata*, this is another song sung to wake up a beloved lady.

Line 2: *Amor* is lacking the final E that would rhyme with *cuore* and complete the rhyme scheme of the first eight lines: abbc addc.

Line 9: *Al Paganini...*, is a dedication to the magazine for which Puccini wrote the song. This and Puccini's signature are his personal joke; probably he never thought anyone would sing them. The singer has some other possibilities: Vocalize on *ah* or *la* or sing the phrase exactly as it was at the beginning of the song.

Musical Background

In 1888 Puccini had seen only his first opera produced, *Le Villi* (named after forest nymphs in a Germanic legend), and he was working on his second, *Edgar*. He was living with a married woman, Elvira, whom he later married, and their son.

Paganini, named for the legendary violinist, was a periodical devoted to music; it was published from 1887–1891. It is hard to believe that such graceful, inspired music was written as a favor to a magazine editor, but that is the case.

Puccini remembered this music and used it again several years later, still in Gb Major, in *La Bohème* (The Bohemian Girl, meaning one who leads a Bohemian lifestyle, 1896). At the end of Act III, Mimí and Rodolfo intend to break off their relationship because he is unable to provide money to treat her illness. While saying goodbye, they simultaneously realize that they do not want to live alone in the winter and that breaking up will be easier in the sunny month of April. Puccini adapted the music of *"Sole e amore"* only slightly for their duet; the music of m28 provides the high Bb that the soprano and tenor sing when they think about the coming of springtime. With the music of m30, the tender mood is interrupted by the quarrel of another couple who are breaking up, Musetta and Marcello. From that point on, the music of *"Sole e amore"* continues to provide an undercurrent that supports the double scene, one couple's reconciliation and another's noisy argument. Critics often cite this scene, one of the marvels of opera, as evidence that opera is better than spoken theater in portraying simultaneous actions.

There is additional detailed information about *"Sole e amore"* in *The Unknown Puccini* by Michael Kaye (New York: Oxford University Press, 1987).

Source

Paganini, No. 23, Anno II (Genoa, 1888), B.25-h.222/39,Milan. Original key: Gb Major.

Sole e amore

Poet unknown (probably Puccini)

Giacomo Puccini
Edited by John Glenn Paton

Il so - le al - le - gra -

men - te bat - te ai tuoi ve - tri. A -

mor pian pian bat - te al tuo cuo - re, e l'u - no e l'al - tro

ⓐ Suggested tempo: ♩ = 92. This is the tempo that Puccini indicated when he re-used this music in *La Bohème*.

ⓑ Puccini indicated the *portamento*, which occurs when a slur connects two different pitches that have two syllables of text. At the end of the first note the voice slides to the pitch of the second note before changing to the second syllable. There is also a *portamento* in m27.

ⓒ The grace notes and the syllable *l'al-* are sung ahead of the beat, taking time from the preceding note.

Translation: The sun cheerfully knocks at your window, love very softly knocks at your heart, and both of them

ⓓ The phrasing slurs come from the composer.

call you. The sun says, "Sleeping one, let me see how beautiful you are." Love says, "Sister, let your first thought be about the one who

loves you."

E l'uccellino...
/e lut:ʃel:li:no/
The Little Bird

Giacomo Puccini (1858–1924)

e   lut:ʃel:li:no kanta sul:la fronda
1. E   l'uccellino   canta sulla   fronda:
And the-little-bird sings on the branch,

dɔrmi traŋkwil:lo bok:kut:ʃa damo:re
2. Dormi tranquillo, boccuccia   d'amore;
"Sleep tranquilly,   dear-mouth of-love

pjɛgala dʒu kwel:la testi:na bjonda
3. Piegala giù   quella testina   bionda,
bend-it down, that   little-head blond,

del:la tua mam:ma pɔːzala sul   kwɔːre
4. Della tua   mamma posala sul   cuore.
of   your mamma put-it   on-the heart."

e   lut:ʃel:li:no kanta su kwel ra:mo
5. E   l'uccellino   canta su quel ramo:
And the-little-bird sings on that   branch,

tante   kozi:ne bɛl:le   imparerai
6. Tante   cosine   belle   imparerai,
"So-many dear-things beautiful you-will-learn,

ma se vor:rai   konoʃ:ʃer kwantio   ta:mo
7. Ma se vorrai   conoscer quant'io   t'amo,
but if you-wanted to-know   how-much-I you-love,

nes:su:no al   mondo potra   dirlo   mai
8. Nessuno al   mondo potrà   dirlo   mai!
no-one   on-the earth   will-be-able to-say-it ever!"

e   lut:ʃel:li:no kantal   tʃɛl sere:no
9. E   l'uccellino   canta al   ciel sereno:
And the-little-bird sings to-the sky   clear,

dɔrmi tezɔ:ro mio kwi sul mio se:no
10. Dormi, tesoro mio, qui sul mio seno.
sleep,   treasure mine, here on my bosom.

Poetic Background

"Sleep, my darling baby. You will never know how much I love you."

Renato Fucini (1843–1921) was Puccini's friend and frequent hunting companion at Torre del Lago. He was well known for his sonnets and wrote many prose works as well.

Musical Background

By 1899 Puccini had established himself as a major composer with the successes of *Manon Lescaut* (1893) and *La Bohème* (1896).

This song, called a *ninna-nanna* (lullaby), is dedicated to a baby. The baby's name was Memmo, a nickname for Guglielmo. His father, Guglielmo Lippi, died before the baby was born, and there was an outpouring of sympathy from his friends, including Puccini, toward the baby and the young mother.

The cover of the first edition was beautifully designed in *Liberty* style, the Italian equivalent of *art nouveau*, and showed a mother and child.

The *staccato* accompaniment figure, many times repeated, resembles the opening of the preceding song, *"Sole e amore."* As in that song, the accompaniment and the melody are so integrated that it is impossible to guess which one occurred to Puccini first.

There is additional detailed information about *"E l'uccellino...."* in *The Unknown Puccini* by Michael Kaye (New York: Oxford University Press, 1987).

Source

"E l'uccellino...., Ninna-nanna (Milan: Ricordi, 1899), Berlin. Dedication *"al bimbino Memmo Lippi."* Original key: D Major.

E l'uccellino...

Renato Fucini

Giacomo Puccini
Edited by John Glenn Paton
(Range: D4–D5)

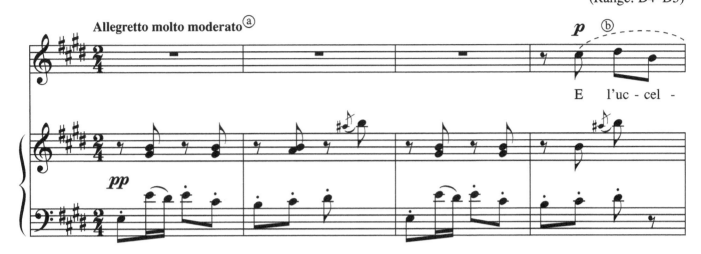

ⓐ Suggested tempo: ♩ = 92.

ⓑ The slur marks come from the composer.

ⓒ Puccini indicated the *portamento* (also in m16 and m32), which occurs when a slur connects two different pitches that have two syllables of text. At the end of the first note the voice slides to the pitch of the second note before changing to the second syllable. In m16 the tone goes up a minor third and then releases to take a breath before going on in m17.

Translation: And the little bird sings on the branch: "Sleep peacefully, sweet little love; lay your head

sti - na bion - da,   del - la tua mam-ma pɔ-sa-la   sul

cuɔ - re.   E l'uc - cel - li - no

can - ta su quel ra - mo: Tan - te co - si - ne

bɛl - le im-pa-re - ra - i,   ma   se vor - rai co -no-scer quan - t'io

on mamma's heart." And the little bird sings on that branch: "You are going to learn so many nice things, but if you
wanted to know how much I

love you, no one on earth could ever tell you!' And the little bird sings to the clear sky: "Sleep, my treasure, here on my bosom."

Un organetto suona per la via
/un organeˈtːto swɔːna per la viːa/
The Street-Organ

Gabriele Sibella (dates unknown)

un organeˈtːto swɔːna per   la viːa
1. **Un organetto suona per   la via,**
   A   barrel-organ sounds through the street,

la mia fineˈstra ɛ aperta e   vjɛn la seːra
2. **La mia finestra è aperta e   vien la sera;**
   — my window is open   and comes the evening;

saːle dai   kampi aˈlːla stantsutːtʃa miːa
3. **Sale dai   campi alla stanzuccia mia**
   rises from-the fields to-the little-room   mine

unaˈːlito   gentil di primaveːra
4. **Un'alito   gentil di primavera.**
   a-light-breeze gentle of spring.

non sɔ   perkɛ mi   trɛːmino i dʒinɔkːki
5. **Non so   perché mi   tremino i ginocchi,**
   not I-know why   of-me tremble   the knees,

non sɔ   perkɛ mi salga il pjanto aʎːʎɔkːki
6. **Non so   perché mi salga il pianto agli occhi:**
   not I-know why   to-me rises the crying to-the eyes:

ɛkːko io kiːno la tɛsta sulːla mia maːno
7. **Ecco, io chino la testa sulla mia mano**
   look, I lean my head on   my hand

e   pɛnso a   te ke sɛi   kozi lontaːno
8. **E   penso a   te che sei   cosí lontano.**
   and think about you that you-are so   far-away.

Poetic Background

"I do not know why the music of a street organ throws me into a melancholy mood, sad because you are far away."

A barrel organ always plays cheerful popular music. But even happy music, for no logical reason, can trigger a sad memory. Guerrini, writing under the name of an imaginary cousin, Lorenzo Stecchetti, published this poem in *Postuma* (1877). Like the text of *"Donna, vorrei morir"* (page 179), this poem compresses an intense mood into eight lines.

Line 1: *Un'organetto* is a mechanical instrument. The operator carries it on a neck strap, leans it on a supporting stick and powers it with a hand crank, hoping to collect money from people going by. The hand crank operates a bellows that sends air through organ pipes; the crank also turns a cylinder, or barrel (like the one in a music box), mounted with pins that open and close the pipes, producing the music. The sound is apt to be a wheezing drone along with a high-pitched melody.

Lines 5 and 6: *mi... i ginocchi... mi... agli occhi*: Italian often uses a reflexive pronoun where English would use a possessive, "my knees...my eyes."

Line 7: *Ecco* is usually said to show something to another person; here, it expresses the surprise that the poet feels about his own mood. *Mia*, not grammatically required in Italian, has been added by the compser

Musical Background

Bringing to life the paradoxical contrast between happy music outdoors and the poet's inner sadness, Sibella wrote music on two levels. Rather than imitating the sound of a barrel organ, the playful *presto* depicts the children who dance around the organ grinder. The tempo slows a little (m3) for the quiet melody of the voice. The initial *presto* returns in m14–15, and again the tempo is slowed by the poet's thoughtful mood, although children still play in the background. At m27 the poet, overwhelmed by sad memories, no longer hears the outer world. The tempo, although slower than *presto*, reflecting how quickly the feelings have arisen. Only for the last line of the poem, *"e penso a te...,"* are there two *rallentando* markings. The composer specified a breath before the final word, *"lontano,"* to underline its pathos. The singer remains lost in thought as the piano postlude tells us that the children are dancing away.

Although Sibella's musical idiom is thoroughly Italian, he achieves a complex and ambiguous expression such as one expects from *lieder* by Schumann or Wolf. One regrets that Sibella published only a few songs in his lifetime.

Source

Quattro romanze per canto, no. 2 (New York: G. Schirmer, 1915). Dedicated *"A Enrico Caruso."* Originally published in two keys, E♭ and F Major.

Un organetto suona per la via

Olindo Guerrini (Lorenzo Stecchetti)

Gabriele Sibella
Edited by John Glenn Paton
(Range: B♭3–F5)

ⓐ "Fast."

Translation: A barrel organ sounds through the street. My window is open and evening is coming. From the

19

cam - pi_al - la stan-zuc-cia mi - a U - n'a-li - to gen -

24

til di pri-ma - vε - ra. Non

rall.

mf   *sf*
        2 pedali

28 *a tempo*

sɔ per-ché mi trɛ - mi - no_i gi - nɔc - chi, Non sɔ per-ché mi

a tempo

sf   *sf*

33

sal - ga_il pian-to_a - gli_ɔc - chi: ɛc - co io

sf

sf   *sf*

fields a gentle spring breeze enters my little room. I do not know why I am trembling, I do not know why tears come to my eyes. Look, I'm

chi - no la tɛ - sta   sul - la mia ma - no   e pen - so a

te,   e pen - so a   te   che sɛi co -

sí   lon - ta - no.

leaning my head on my hand and thinking about you, who are so far away.

Madrigale
Madrigal

Gabriele Sibella (dates unknown)

madɔnːna io vaːmo e   tatːtʃo
1. **Madonna, io v'amo e   taccio;**
   My-lady,   I you-love and am-silent;

vel   pwɔ dʒuraːramoːre
2. **ve'l   può giurar Amore,**
   to-you-it can swear Love,

ke tantɛ   fɔːko in me kwantin vɔi gjatːtʃo
3. **Che tant'è   foco in me quant'in voi ghiaccio.**
   that as-much-is fire in me as   in you ice.

e   sio non   ɔːzo diːre
4. **E   s'io non   oso dire**
   And if-I do-not dare to-say

lintɛnso mio martiːre
5. **L'intenso mio martire,**
   the-intense my suffering,

nol fɔ per salvar me   mal vɔstroːnoːre
6. **No'l fo per salvar me,   ma'l vostro onore.**
   not-it I-do to save   myself, but-the your   honor.

io vi pɔrto nel   kɔːre
7. **Io vi porto nel   core;**
   I you carry in-the heart;

da vɔi vjɛn lalta   spɛːme el   gran deziːre
8. **Da voi vien l'alta speme e'l   gran desire,**
   From you comes the-high hope   and-the great desire

e   mertʃɛ vɔstra viːvo in fjamːme atːtʃeːzo
9. **E   grace vostra vivo in fiamme acceso:**
   and mercy yours I-live in flames   burning:

vorːria   sɛntsa parlar esːserinteːzo
10. **Vorria   senza parlar esser inteso.**
    I-would-like without speaking to-be understood.

Poetic Background

"I am burning with love for you, but I shall never speak of it."

A poet whose name has been forgotten is addressing a woman who is far above him in social rank. In the courtly life of the early 1500s, marriages were political unions, not love matches. It was expected that a married woman might receive the secret admiration of one or more lovers. In this case, the lady has shown no sympathy for the young man. Perhaps she has admonished him to keep silent.

Madrigale means a type of short poem, usually idyllic and amorous, written in lines of varying lengths. The term may come from a Latin word *matricale,* "in the mother tongue" (meaning Italian, not Latin). This poem is a typical madrigal of the 1500s, with ten lines, each containing seven or 11 syllables, and an irregular rhyme scheme ending with a rhymed couplet of 11-syllable lines.

Line 1: *Madonna* is a term of address for a lady of high station (also, but not in this case, for the Virgin Mary). *V'amo*: the pronoun of respectful address is second person plural. *Taccio* comes from *tacere,* to be silent.

Line 2: *ve'l*: a contraction of *ve il.* In modern Italian: *A voi può giurarlo Amore.* Love itself is called as a witness.

Line 3: *foco in* contains a diphthong between words (synalepha) in which /i/ is the main vowel, being in the essential word *in.* The original madrigal confirms this, because in that text the /o/ is elided entirely: *foc'in.*

Line 6: *No'l fo*: in modern Italian, *Non lo faccio. Vostro onore*: her honor would be defiled if the poet told others about his love.

Line 9: *mercé vostra* can be understood two ways, like its English equivalent, "thanks to you." The poet might be blaming the lady for the torments of love, or he might be thanking her because he is happy to be enflamed with love.

Musical Background

At the head of this song Sibella placed a motto of six notes, attributed to Costanzo Festa (circa 1490–1545). Festa was among the first group of composers who established the contrapuntal madrigal as the predominant form of secular music for rest of the 1500s. He sang and composed music at the royal court of France before joining the papal choir in Rome. He composed masses and motets for the church, as well as secular madrigals. Festa's *"Madonna, io v'amo"* was a madrigal for three voices published in 1537.

Some of Sibella's contemporaries published versions of early music that were falsified by drastically inappropriate harmonies and dynamics. Others composed forgeries and passed them off as genuine works of earlier composers. Using a more honest approach, Sibella took a text and a bit of melody from an ancient work, acknowledged their source, and used them to create something new. In fact, he borrowed only a few measure of melody and adapted them freely.

Instead of the three contrapuntal voices of Festa's composition, Sibella prefers a solo voice supported by the full chords of a pianoforte, the typical Romantic instrument. Renaissance composers told us nothing at all about dynamics, but Sibella demands a wide range of dynamics and specifies them for each phrase. The result is a compelling, passionate song that has a halo of antiquity about it.

Sources

(1) *Madrigale* (New York: G. Schirmer, 1921). Original key: G minor.

(2) *"Madonna, io v'am' e taccio"* in Costanzo Festa *Opera Omnia,* vol. 7, edited by Albert Seay (Stuttgart: Hänssler-Verlag, 1977).

Madrigal

Unknown, early 1500s

Gabriele Sibella
Edited by John Glenn Paton
(Range: D4–F5)

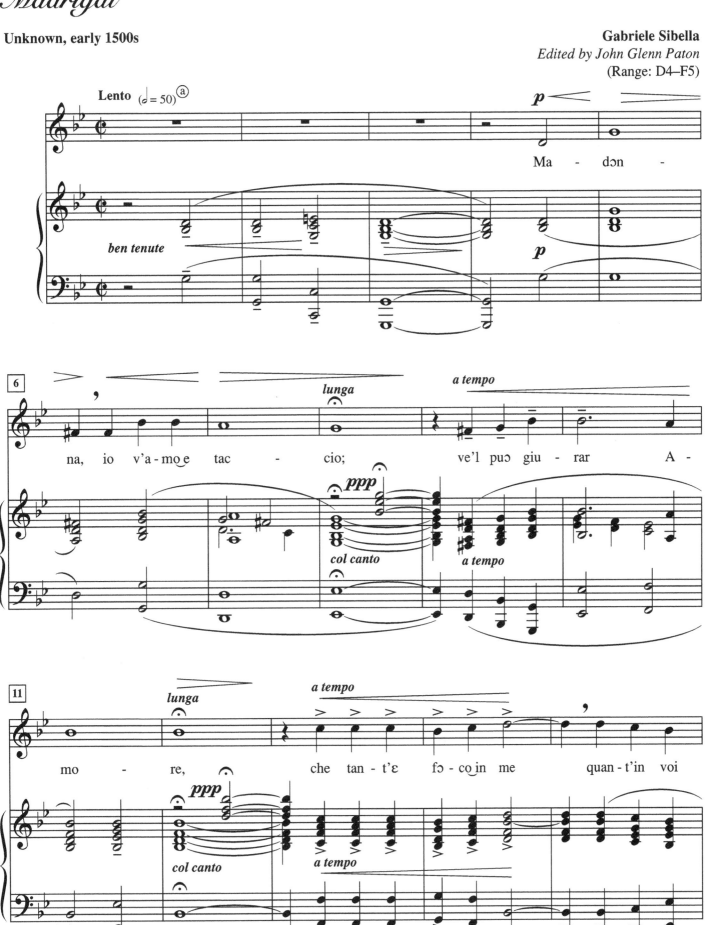

ⓐ "Slow." Notice that there should be two beats (half-notes) per measure, which will keep the song from becoming too slow.

Translation: My lady, I love you in silence. Love itself will witness that there is as much fire in me as there is

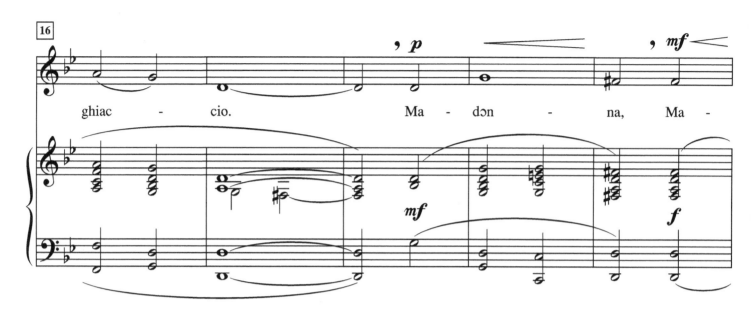

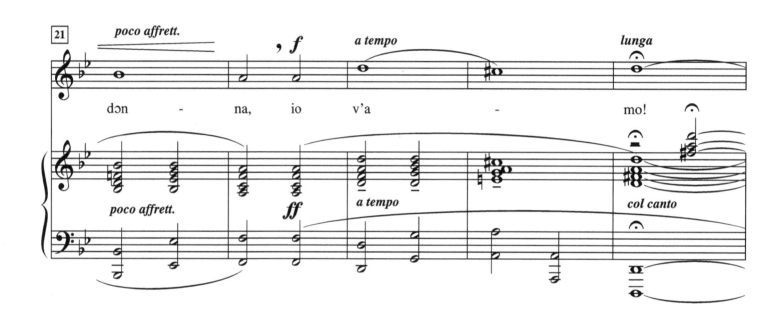

ice in your heart. If I do not dare to speak of my intense pain, it is not

for my own sake but for the sake of your honor. You are in my heart; from you I draw both high hope and great desire, and thanks to you I live in burning flames.

I would like you to understand me without my speaking.

Musical Terms in Italian

The stressed syllable is usually next-to-last. Stress on some other syllable (not shown in normal printing) is indicated here by an accent over the vowel (à, é, í, ú) or by the use of the phonetic symbols ɛ or ɔ, which occur only in stressed syllables.

accel., accelerando	becoming gradually faster
adagio	a slow tempo, faster than *largo* and slower than *andante*
affrett., affrettando	hurrying, speeding up
agitato	agitated
allarg., allargando	becoming slower and broader
allegretto	a little lively (slower than *allegro*)
allegro	lively, cheerful, quick or fast
a guisa di liuto	like a lute
a mezza voce	in half voice, softly
ancora	again, still, more
andante	at a walking pace (in pre-Romantic music), slowly (in Romantic music) (lit., walking, going)
andantino	moderately slow (either slower or faster than *andante*)
animato	animated, spirited
a piacere	slowly, not in strict rhythm (lit., at pleasure)
a pɔco a pɔco	little by little
appassionato	passionately
armonioso	harmoniously
arpeggiato	arpeggiated, as broken chords
assai	very
a tɛmpo	in time; either resuming a previous tempo or beginning a tempo after unmeasured music
bɛn	well
brillante	brilliant, brilliantly
calando	becoming slower and softer (lit., lowering gradually)
carezzévole	caressingly
col canto	with the voice (an instruction to the pianist)
colla voce	the same as *col canto*
con accɛnto	with accentuation
con affetto	with affection
con ànima	with soul, expressively
con brio	with brilliance
con calore	with heat
con eleganza	with elegance
con fɔrza	with force
con fuɔco	with fire
con grazia	with grace
con mɔto	with motion, with movement
con 8va, con ottava	with octave doubling
con passione	with passion
con tutta forza	with full strength
cresc., crescɛndo	growing, becoming louder
deciso	decisively, boldly
dim., diminuɛndo	diminishing, gradually becoming softer
dolce, dolcemente	sweetly
dolciss., dolcissimo	very sweetly
e, ed	and
espandɛndosi	expanding (itself)
espress., espressivo	expressively
gaio	gaily
giusto	appropriate, not too much or too little
grande	large, much
grandioso	grandly
gruppetto	in early Baroque music, a trill
largamente	broadly
larghetto	somewhat broadly, faster than *largo*
legato	smoothly connected (lit., bound)
lɔco	in place, as written (after a passage played an octave higher)
lunga, lungo	long
marcato	marked, slightly emphasized and separated
moderato	moderately, between *andante* and *allegretto*
molto	very
morɛndo	dying away, getting softer
opp., oppure	or (to indicate an alternative note or notes)
ossía	or (the same as *oppure*)
parlato	spoken, in a speaking manner (the same as *parlando, parlante*)
piú	more
pɔco, un pɔco	little, a little
pɔi	then
primo tɛmpo	the same tempo as at the beginning, abbr. *1ᵐᵒ tɛmpo*
quasi	as if
rall., rallentando	relenting, becoming gradually slower
riprendɛndo	resuming (a previous tempo)
rit.	either *ritenuto* or *ritardando*
ritardando	becoming gradually slower
ritenuto	at a slower tempo (suddenly, not gradually)
scherz., scherzando	playfully
sɛmpre	always
sf., sfz., sforzato	with a sudden, strong accent, (lit., forced)
smorz., smorzando	dying away, being dampened (in sound)
sonɔro	sonorously, with good sound
sospeso	hesitating (lit., suspended)
sost., sostenuto	sustained
stacc., staccato	short, detached
stentato	labored, done with effort
tɛmpo	speed
tempo primo, Iᴼ	in the former tempo
tɛmpo di valse	waltz tempo (silent final E, as in French)
ten., tenuto	held, at least for the note's full value
trillo	trill or, in early Baroque music, a rapid repetition of single pitch
vivo	lively, spirited

Phonemes of Italian

IPA Symbols	Symbol Names	Similar English Sounds
1. [i]	Lower-case I	ma<u>ch</u>ine
2. [e]	Lower-case E	ch<u>a</u>otic
3. [ɛ]	Epsilon	r<u>e</u>d
4. [a]	Lower-case A	f<u>a</u>ther
5. [u]	Lower-case U	tr<u>u</u>th
6. [o]	Lower-case O	<u>o</u>ceanic
7. [ɔ]	Open O	<u>ou</u>ght
8. [j]	Lower-case J	<u>y</u>es
9. [w]	Lower-case W	<u>w</u>et
10. [m]	Lower-case M	<u>m</u>ime
11. [n]	Lower-case N	<u>n</u>oon
12. [ɲ]	Left-tail N	(none in English)
13. [ŋ]	Eng	si<u>ng</u>
14. [l]	Lower-case L	<u>l</u>augh
15. [ʎ]	Turned Y	(none in English)
16. [r] or [ɾ]	Lower-case R Fishhook R	(trill R, none in English) me<u>rr</u>y (formal, tap R)
17. [p]	Lower-case P	<u>p</u>ie
18. [b]	Lower-case B	<u>b</u>uy
19. [t]	Lower-case T	<u>t</u>oo
20. [d]	Lower-case D	<u>d</u>o
21. [k]	Lower-case K	<u>c</u>ap
22. [g]	Lower-case G	<u>g</u>ap
23. [f]	Lower-case F	<u>f</u>at
24. [v]	Lower-case V	<u>v</u>at
25. [s]	Lower-case S	<u>S</u>ue
26. [z]	Lower-case Z	<u>z</u>oo
27. [ʃ]	Esh	<u>sh</u>oe
28. [ts]	T-S affricate	si<u>ts</u> up
29. [dz]	D-Z affricate	a<u>dds</u> on
30. [tʃ]	T-Esh affricate	<u>ch</u>urch
31. [dʒ]	D-Yogh affricate	<u>j</u>udge